Witch's
Guide
to
Wands

The Witch's Guide to Wands

A Complete Botanical, Magical, and Elemental Guide to Making, Choosing, and Using the Right Wand

GYPSEY ELAINE TEAGUE

WEISERBOOKS
San Francisco, CA / Newburyport, MA

This edition first published in 2015 by Weiser Books

Red Wheel/Weiser, LLC
With offices at:
665 Third Street, Suite 400
San Francisco, CA 94107
www.redwheelweiser.com

ISBN: 978-1-57863-570-2

Library of Congress Cataloging-in-Publication Data is available on request.

Cover design by Jim Warner
Interior by Deborah Dutton
Typeset in Goudy Oldstyle and Goudy Text

Printed in the United States of America
EBM

10 9 8 7 6 5 4 3 2 1

Contents

Foreword

I am a longtime witch, seer, and root worker of more than thirty years. So, I am no newcomer to spiritual, magical, and mystical work. As such, every now and again I will meet a teacher, experience a ritual, encounter a tradition, or review a book that contributes to witchcraft and magic in a way that has depth, wisdom, power, and practicality. When this happens, I do a "happy dance," and I get increased enthusiasm for where witchery is moving and its usefulness to the world.

The book you hold in your hands is inspiring such a hopeful response in me. So, this is not a mere "foreword"; it is a declaration of usefulness to the work therein. It is a call to action for the spirit of the tool we call "wand"—its uses and the working of woods in its magic. Gypsey Elaine Teague shows us the ways to work metals too, but woods are her focus, since they have occupied a place in magic far before the advent of fire and metallurgy. A wood wand is a means to encounter the roots, trunk, and branches of a magic tree that grows from the earth prior to human hands. It is a means to manipulate the forces of magic through an ally (the tree and its woods) that have been shaping the forces of heaven (sun, stars, planets, and moon) and ancestry (human and other) through the unifying forces of the tree for millions of years. Who is better at bringing the powers of above, below, and the horizon than the tree?

So, this foreword is more than a recommendation. It is an invitation. Read this book and work its contents; pass it on to others who seek to work the ways of the wand in witchery. Finally, through the agency of this book, the work of the wand is receiving the attention it deserves as a specific tool in the magic of the witch! I am hopeful that readers will see the power and application of the wand as a magical tool the way our ancestors did, and will seek and secure the potent powers of the woods of the wand for the ways of witchery and make good magic happen in the world!

As a witch with more than thirty years of experience practicing and teaching the craft, this book will be on my recommended reading list. Why, you might ask? Well, for the following reasons. This book:

- Gives wands the attention they deserve as a special item in the witch's toolbox.

- Gives an introduction to the names, spirits, and attributes of the woods for the wand in a way that has not been done in the past.

- Profiles the full anatomy of a wand and its applications to accessing, shaping, and channeling magical forces to a forecasted, projected, and desired outcome.

- Demonstrates an admirable love and commitment to the wand, wood, and their power like I have never witnessed in previous books and teachings.

We have all heard of magic wands in the books, movies, and teachings of our media, magical practices, and traditions. But they are often overgeneralized or embedded in a cadre of implements without attention and honor given to them as the powerful tool they are. Teague treats the subject of wands as a specific magical practice and tradition. This approach is fresh, respectful, and useful. After all, if wands are only a side note, why should we respect and use them? Teague demonstrates that these tools and their spiritual powers should have their unique and specific place on the magical stage.

Wands have captured our attention in movies, lore, and practices. But, have they had their place in our attention in a way that shows their anatomy and application? No, I doubt they have! In the book you hold, Teague seduces us into the allure of wands while informing us of their usefulness. She brings our attention to the wisdom of "there is a partnership between the witch and the wand." This relationship can only be discovered and cultivated through intimate partnership. So, to enhance this, she gives a structure to the formal introduction between the witch and the wood for the wand—the order, family, genus, and species, as well as the Janka hardness scale, energy, elements, Celtic ogham (where applicable), and Gods and Goddesses represented—as a means for the human magic worker to meet the spirit of the wood on a dancing floor of conscious change and mediation of magical influence. She does this using the feel of a family member introducing you to fellow family at a reunion. She also does this as a craftswoman welcoming you to her craft and her group. Invite the wand to your altar. Work its power for magical influence. Seek and find its mysteries. Find the ways of the witch in the working of the wand.

—Orion Foxwood

Introduction

The wand chooses the witch; the witch does not choose the wand.

Two women, one about sixty and a younger one in her teens, enter a tent at a pagan event. The small sign on a table by the entrance says CANES AND WANDS FOR ALL OCCASIONS. They are a few steps behind a man in his late twenties. The man is wearing jeans, boots, and a T-shirt that says across the front DO AS YE SHALL, RECEIVE AS YE WILL—THRICE. The young man walks up to the back table where a woman sits reading. She looks up and brushes a loose strand of blonde hair out of her face and says, "Good morning. Cane or wand?"

"I'm being threatened," he says as he looks around the tent. "I need protection."

"Protection," the blonde responds, and the other two watch from the edge of the tent. "Let me see what we have then."

She pulls a few long, slender silk bags from under a glass display case and spreads them out on the table.

"One of these should do the trick," she smiles.

The man passes his hand over the bags. He touches none of them but stops at one toward his right, second from the end.

"This one," he declares.

"A good choice," the blonde smiles again. She carefully wraps the bag in white paper and places it in a small box, never looking inside. "Fig," she says as she hands the wrapped wand to her customer. "Fourteen inches long, double knot and single ring. A very good choice." She bows slightly and he returns the bow.

The customer doesn't ask how she knew what was in the bag and she doesn't explain that even though the silk bags appear identical, each has a small difference that can be seen if looked for. He would use the wand to protect himself against whatever was challenging him. It would be a good fit.

After the man leaves, the two women approach the counter. The blonde looks up and smiles again.

"Cane or wand?" she asks.

"First wand," the older woman with gray-streaked hair says quietly.

"For this young lady?" the blonde inquires.

"Yes," the older woman replies. "Initiation tonight."

The little girl never looks up. She stares at the ground unsure of what to do. She has been studying for over a year and is to be initiated tonight and admitted to the coven. Afraid to do anything incorrect this weekend, the girl has kept to herself and tried to stay out of trouble. She had succeeded so far, she thought, though the day was still young.

"First wand," the blonde woman mused. "We must offer a good selection then." She began placing long velvet wand bags across her table, covering almost five feet of the counter.

When she was finished, the woman behind the counter addressed the young woman with her head bowed.

"The wand chooses the witch," the blonde said. "The witch does not choose the wand."

"Ma'am?" the girl looked up suddenly, thinking the woman was reciting something from Harry Potter.

"Place your hand over the bags," the blonde instructed. "Pass your hand slowly over each until the wand that is yours tells you."

The young girl looked at her High Priestess inquiringly.

"You can do it," the older woman assured her. "Pass your hand over the bags one by one. You'll know when it's right."

The teenager began at her left and passed her right hand over each bag, holding it there for a few seconds and then continuing. At the end of the long row the girl began pushing the bags slightly toward the blonde across from her.

"I'm getting nothing from these," she said softly.

When the field was down to six bags, the girl began again. Slowly, and this time more deliberately, she passed her right hand over each bag. Finally she stopped and pointed.

"This one," she said.

"We'll take this one," the older woman replied. She paid for the wand and they left the shop.

Purpleheart, thought the woman as she put the others away. Single flute at handle. Triple band at head.

The wand would give the young girl courage and self-sacrifice. She would carry that wand for forty years through a number of covens until as High Priest-ess of her own coven she would choose a bloodwood wand the night before her Croning.

Turning back toward the front of the tent, the blonde greeted a man and his wife.

"Cane or wand?" she asked.

Purpose

This book began as two seemingly unrelated meetings in two states at two separate times of the year. I am a woodworker. When I was younger, I built houses with my uncle and then had a company that built residential and light commercial buildings. I have also logged in New Hampshire during a very cold stretch of winter and poured steel in a foundry during a very hot summer. These jobs trained me to create.

Three years ago at Florida Pagan Gathering I was discussing wands that I turned on a lathe in my small woodshop with some Elders and prac-ticing witches. I had about two dozen wands of various woods for sale, and customers would come into my tent and hold them, finding one that spoke to them and had the requisite energy for their use. One customer in particular said he liked black walnut, but lately it had been giving him trouble when casting healing spells. He eventually found a very nice white willow wand that he felt would do the job and left smiling. I didn't think anything more of that incident until later in the year when I was talking to some students in the landscape architecture graduate program in the building where I work.

I'm the Branch Head of the Gunnin Architecture Library at Clemson University and also a faculty member in the landscape architecture program. I was sitting with some students toward the end of the semester, discussing their work and what they'd called out—a professional term referring to the plants, trees, and shrubs chosen for a specific design.

The owner of the property in the design liked nut trees and had a number on the property. One was a medium-sized black walnut. He said that he wanted the house to have a garden, and the walnut tree would give the plants enough shade to keep them from burning. He specifically mentioned having tomatoes and some other vegetables. It was then that I offered a critical problem with the black walnut: the chemical juglone, released through a process known as allelopathy, the discharge of one species of plant inhibiting or restricting the growth of another, kills or damages many plants around the tree—especially tomatoes and peppers. I also commented that the bark or pollen of the black walnut can cause skin problems for those who are susceptible to such issues.

That's when I remembered the first conversation in my tent in Ocala, Florida, a few months earlier. The witch in question had tried to use a poisonous wand to heal. I also then understood why the white willow wand was the one that had spoken to him. For the next month I thought on this, and I realized after looking into a number of reference books that even though we go to great lengths to explain to our witchlings how to find and prepare their own wand for use, we almost completely ignore the wood it's made of. You would not use a holly wand for a new moon ritual any more than you would use an ebony one for a full moon. If you want strength, then you would use oak and reserve the willow for resilience and survival spells.

This book came about after these two meetings. Here, you will find organic and inorganic wands. The first, and largest, part of the book covers organic materials—woods. Most are trees, but some shrubs, roots, grasses, and vines are also included since they may be large enough to work as wands. Also in this section will be a discussion on hybrid wands, those curious mixings of two or more woods fashioned for a purpose so unique that a standard wand may not fit the bill. I look at the specifics of the wood: its grain, color, hardness, and how it turns on a lathe and polishes. I also discuss the properties of each tree or shrub and comment on specific rituals associated with that particular wand.

The second part covers inorganic materials—metal. With the growing interest in Steampunk Magic, more wands are being crafted from brass and bronze. I take into account the shape, hardness of the metal, and magical properties. I also recommend specific spells and rituals for each permutation.

The third part of the book will be a short discussion on the wands of the Harry Potter franchise of books and theme parks. With the growing interest in the young wizard and other wand makers claiming to place phoenix feathers, dragon heartstrings, or unicorn hairs in their wands, I think an explanation of whether or not Ms. Rowling got it right when she wrote about the powers of the wands and those who wield them is worthwhile.

While no book is exhaustive on this subject due to the number of woods and materials out there, I've included enough local materials and locally available exotic materials to give the reader a knowledgeable choice in the matter of wands and their uses. Only the end result by the user will show whether I've succeeded.

Wand Basics

One simply does not serve soup with a butter knife!

Wands. Without them we would be missing a great part of our tool kit. Scott Cunningham says in his book *Wicca: A Guide for the Solitary Practitioner* that you can even use a wooden dowel purchased from a hardware store as a wand. While that is true, and any piece of wood works under general conditions, it really is important to know the source of your material and the conditions under which that piece was obtained.

Another staple reference book of witchcraft is Raymond Buckland's *Complete Book of Witchcraft*. Here, Buckland says that the power of the wand comes from the witch and not necessarily from the wand. I agree with that to a point. While you may practice magic naked with your index finger, it is important that you understand the power of the tools if you are going to use them. Therefore, I believe you should choose your wand more carefully than either Buckland or Cunningham suggest.

There is a partnership between the witch and the wand. Any witch who has his or her favorite or working wand will tell you the energy generated between the wand and the witch is significant and prevalent. Wands are like shoes or jeans or shirts or your favorite little black dress. When it's right, it's just right and you know it. Therefore, when you craft your first or third or ninth wand and it doesn't respond to you, don't worry. A piece of wood in the wild or in the lumberyard is very different once you begin talking to it and crafting it. Think of building your relationship with your wand as dating. You may go out on a number of dates with a number of different people before you get the right spark. And even then, after marriage the spark may still not be right. So it is with your wand. Work for the spark, but don't expect overnight success.

For a more detailed approach to wands, I recommend Dorothy Morrison's book *The Craft: A Witch's Book of Shadows*. Morrison goes into detail about the particular properties of wands and explains that it's just not about wandering aimlessly, gathering sticks and twigs in the hopes that one might become a wand. She explains the harvesting of the wand, which I think is an essential part of all witch's training. She also goes into detail about personalizing your wand after you have procured the material. These are all important aspects of the training young witches should receive.

Most authors agree that a wand should be approximately the length from the tip of your middle finger to the crook of your arm. This makes it the length of your hand and forearm. To me, that is a little long, and I personally like a shorter wand of about fourteen inches. But this book is not about length as much as it's about substance, so I'm not going to lay down some grand law to follow in making your wand.

It is important to understand that there are wands and then there are *wands*. With the popularity of Harry Potter, wands have gained an elevated status in pop culture. An entire generation has grown up with a renewed sense of wand appreciation not seen since Disney's *Cinderella* of 1960. Now, not just witches and fairy godmothers wield wands—every young child who has read Rowling's books and envisioned him- or herself as a wizard at Hogwarts has a wand in hand. Unfortunately, these same children grow up not understanding the difference between a play stick called a wand and a wand as held by an actual magician. These children and adults believe that you can put a phoenix feather or a unicorn hair into a wand to gain more power against the Dark Lord. So is the way of popular culture, I suppose. However, for a detailed explanation of the wands of the Harry Potter books and how they correspond to the characters they chose, see the section later in this book.

There is a saying that one simply does not serve soup with a butter knife. This means we do not use the same tool for every occasion. In construction, people say that if all you have is a hammer, then everything begins to look like a nail. That is very true with wands. If we have one and only one wand, then I believe we can only do spells or rituals that accommodate that one particular wand. You can't successfully perform a vast array of spells with a single wand any more than you can cook and serve an entire feast with a single butter knife. You must have more than one. This is a book of choices.

This book is also a book of construction. Each wand discussed will include how the wand was made. The lathe is just a tool; but then again, so is a wand. Some wands should be crafted at specific times and days of the month or even the year. If you cast a variety of spells and perform a plethora of rituals, then you should, and I say "should" since I don't want to be accused of being dogmatic, have a wand for each area within which you are working. And not all wands should be from a single material. Wands are like anything else you use. If you must have two or three traits for a spell, then why not turn a wand out of two or three different woods?

Wands are also like batteries; there is a positive end and a negative end. I polled my witch community to ask how they use their wands. Over 90 percent said they use the pointy end only, which we will refer to as the head of the wand. A good friend added that if the wand is unidirectional—that is, one end is pointier than the other—then he will only cast with the head, but if he has a wand that has no head, then he considers it a bidirectional wand and either end will do. I agree with that wholeheartedly for him, but I contend that even if there is a head and a base, you still may use both ends.

From left to right: base, shaft, head

A battery is powerful from both ends, and you must connect a wire to each end to draw the current from it. So is it with a wand. However, do not think of the metaphor of the battery as a discussion of good and evil. The positive and negative ends of the battery are just two sides of the same force, like two sides of the same coin. Neither is better or worse. They are used in conjunction to be a complete whole. Sort of like the yin and yang of the power you are holding.

If you are using a peach wand, the properties are both positive—love and fertility—as well as negative—exorcism. For love and fertility you would hold the base and direct your energy with the head. If you were working an exorcism or banishing spell, then you would need more of a negative power, the power of the base, and therefore you would turn the wand around and hold the head and use the base.

The section of the wand between the base and the head is the shaft. Some bases are ornamental or embellished. In a metal wand, the base may be large and fashioned around a crystal. In an organic wand, the base may be finely tooled or turned and marked with sigils or other symbols important to its user. Therefore, the base may extend far into the shaft, but that is what the wand dictates.

Let's now look at how we make the wands and the space we occupy while doing that.

Preparing Your Workspace

The other day a friend asked me if anyone could make a wand. My answer was both yes and no. While anyone can make a drumstick, which is really what a wand looks like to most people, not just anyone can make a wand for someone else. Also, an individual may wander through the woods and choose a piece of fallen branch that suits him or her, but that doesn't mean that any branch may become a wand for anyone.

There are a few who craft wands. Some do it all by hand, some by hand and machine, and some by other methods. The results are usually the same: a beautiful tool meant for a specific individual, even if that individual has not yet been chosen by the wand. But what does it take to go from raw materials to a finished product capable of casting energy both out and in for years and decades to come? It takes a tool specifically fitted to the energy requirements of a single person. You may gravitate to the perfect wand the first time you find a wand maker; in some instances that choice may take years—or it may never happen. Those are the odds of wands.

One of my graduate students once asked if I took apprentices. I said yes. Then I added a caveat that the individual would have to be an Elder in a pagan tradition, path, or system *and* have twenty years of experience working with woods and tools. My student asked if five years of shop would get him in the door. That's when I explained not *and/or* but *and*. I said I could take the five years, but he would still need to be an Elder, or at least a senior practitioner. I knew he was not pagan, and he knew it too. I told him that perhaps next year, when I expand my boxes and display business, I may be able to hire him since I know he's quite diligent at what he does and knowledgeable of building wood properties. But he's not a witch.

When I start in my shop, the first thing I do is throw up a circle. I am using the term "throw up" because I don't perform a full-blown circle for shop work. I cast with my finger in a modified Georgian fashion. I ask the Gods and Goddesses of wood, creativity, and magic to watch over me and keep me safe. I also promise that my wands will be made with the proper respect to the woods and those who will ultimately use them. I think that is important when dealing with a magical tool.

I think this is part of the reason not just anyone can make a wand. A wand is a sacred tool and should be created in a sacred way. Now the second part of creating the wand is what happens inside the circle.

I make certain that the wood used is purchased, donated, or cut with reverence. If I am the one harvesting the wood, I will talk to the tree, touch which pieces need to be cut, and then with permission trim the pieces. I usually have ten to twenty different woods drying at any time in my wood racks so that I'm always behind in turning wands. Since it takes at least a year to thoroughly dry cut wood, there is a lot of downtime between the harvesting and the finished product. Some wands I'll turn when the wood is still green just to see what will happen. I use these as teaching wands when I give seminars and panels, since they will ultimately warp slightly, or in some cases significantly.

After gathering and drying the wood, the process is pretty much the same. I first cut a blank. This is a piece of wood that's $^3/_4$ inch x $^3/_4$ inch x 16 inches. Next, I drill a small hole at each end, slightly rounding one end to fit in my chuck and not split the blank, and then I turn the wand. If the piece starts out curved or irregularly shaped—this can happen with shrubs and vines such as rosemary, wisteria, or poison ivy—then I do everything by hand, starting with a very coarse sandpaper and working my way down to a very fine grit. The more I do of either, the more I learn. I now know that rosemary can be worked with a belt sander to a certain point since the outer bark is hard and rough. Rosemary also responds best if it is worked during a lightning storm. I don't know why, it just does. Poison ivy must be worked with a rasp plane because of the dust, and if it is still dripping, as the last pieces were, then extra caution must be used. You can find a rasp plane at your local hardware store. It has what looks like a cheese grater on the bottom, and it's used for quick planing when a flat, smooth surface is not necessary.

One more comment on dust. When sanding wands on a lathe, there is a lot of wood dust. It is anywhere from coarse to fine, and it collects on everything. I make certain I have a very clean lathe when I begin a wand

and then I collect the wood dust in jars. These fine particles are excellent for ritual work when you need an added push. Some of the better wood dusts are ebony, holly, lignum vitae, black walnut, bay, purpleheart, and bloodwood/satine. You may burn the dust on a charcoal in your brazier instead of incense, and the power of the wood will benefit what you are trying to accomplish in circle.

When I am done working for the night, I take down the circle as I clean the floor. I have breathing problems from past work experiences, so I keep my shop as clean as I can. As I dust and vacuum the floor and other areas and move the lathe or other tools back where they are stored, I close and release the energy.

Once a wand is finished, it is placed in its own bag for storage. These are wands that have no outside influence. I try to keep them as clean, pure, and free of external energy as possible.

I've been asked if I sell wands online. I usually won't. If I know the individual well and he or she tells me the kinds of wood that are of interest, I'll send about a half dozen choices. If one works, the customer pays me and sends the rest back. Obviously, I don't do that for everyone. I would have hundreds of wands traveling all over the country daily. I have said it before, and I will close this section with this: The wand chooses the witch. Therefore, you must have the wand and the witch in the same space at the same time. I am fortunate that I have the time and inclination to travel to many shows throughout the year.

In conclusion, find a wand maker you trust. Then allow your wand to find you. Both you and the wand will be happier and more successful for the experience.

Part One
Organic Wands—Woods

People love chopping wood. In this activity one immediately sees results.

—ALBERT EINSTEIN

Wood. It's the generic term that we all use to denote anything from trees to shrubs to building materials. It's the fallback when we can't think of what else to call something large, green, vascular, and organic. We go to the woods. We build our houses with wood. In golf, even though now they are made of alloys, the fairway clubs are called woods. We create plywood from other pieces of wood. However, how many of us actually think of the kinds of wood that are lumped together to create plywood?

When we go to the lumberyard, do we consider that the framing wood we purchase for home projects are usually No. 2 or No. 3 pine? Do most of us even know the difference between yellow and white pine? Do we realize that the ponderosa or western yellow pine is larger and slower growing than its cousin the white pine?

And what about the oaks, another multiple species? Do we realize that red and white oaks are both specific types and generalizations of groupings? There are over six hundred different oaks, but when we go to the craft stores, there is only one sign for red oak. And without looking at the leaves and/or bark, it's impossible to tell the difference between the types. Even stores that stock specialty woods call their oak *Quercus rubra* or red oak. Nothing more—just red oak.

As witches, we are very specific about our spells and our rituals. We demand the finest tinctures and oils, the purest herbs, and if possible, we grow everything ourselves. We fill our bookshelves with tomes that explain in detail each and every ingredient that will go into our brazier or cauldron, but when it comes to wands, the books usually say, "walk among the trees and find a piece of wood that suits you." Really? "Suits you?" Would you dress for ritual in whatever suits you without some research or discussion? I think not, although I have been wrong in that thought before.

Order

When we begin looking at wood we must identify what is usually referred to as some form of vascular plant. The highest classification, or taxonomy, that we will work from in this book is the order. The order of a large number of the vascular plants is *Fagales*. This order encompasses many of the best-known trees that we derive our working stock from to create our wands.

Family

In the case of oak the family is *Fagaceae*, which is the beech family. Some of the other families that we will work with are *Betulaceae*, the birch family; *Casuarinaceae*, the she-oak family; *Juglandaceae*, the walnut family; *Myricaceae*, the bayberry family; and *Nothofagaceae*, the southern beech family. We will also look at subfamilies such as the *Caesalpinioideae*, which has as one of its members the heart tree.

Genus

Now back to the red and white oak. The next level under family is genus. The genus of oak is *Quercus*. All oaks will start with *Quercus* and then differentiate by species.

Species

Earlier I talked about red and white oaks and how there were a number of different types of each. That is an example of species. The species will give the type of oak, so a *Quercus nigra*, or water oak, which is a white oak will be different than a *Quercus marilandica*, or blackjack oak, which is a red oak.

What does this mean to a witch who is looking for a white or red oak? It means that there are specific differences between the two, and there are easy ways to tell those differences in the wild.

The last area in preparation to beginning your reading is how the trees and shrubs are listed in groupings. For this I am deferring to Carl E. Whitcomb's *Know It and Grow It II: A Guide to the Identification and Use of Landscape Plants*, which as far as I am concerned is the definitive book on trees and shrubs. Although not as widely used as Michael A. Dirr's *Manual of Woody Landscape Plants: Their Identification, Ornamental Characteristics, Culture, Propagation and Lives*, I find that it is a better guide. Therefore, I shall break the organic part of this book into the following sections: Deciduous Trees; Deciduous Shrubs, Vines, Grasses, and Roots; Broadleaf Evergreens; and Coniferous Trees.

Format of Individual Choices

There must be some commonalities and structure to any book, and this book is no different. Each entry will begin with the common name of the tree in English. Beneath that will be the order, family, genus, and species. Next comes the Janka hardness scale rating, if available (more on this in a moment), followed by the metaphysical properties of the wood or metal—the energy (masculine or feminine), corresponding elements (earth, air, wind, and fire), the corresponding Celtic ogham (if applicable), and finally any Gods or Goddesses attributed to the wood.

A brief discussion of the general characteristics of each plant will follow, and I will explain its benefits, locales, reasons for use, and reasons for caution.

A note on the Janka scale for those who are unfamiliar: The Janka hardness scale is performed by pressing a .444-inch steel ball into a sample of wood until one half of the ball is embedded. Using a specific formula, a rating number is derived from 0 to approximately 5,000. The higher the number, the harder the wood. This rating is usually in relation to flooring and how well a wood will hold up to dents, scratches, and general wear and tear. Another good reason to look at the Janka is because most wands will be turned on a lathe and the hardness of the wood is important to the tools and finishings necessary.

Most of the wooden wands are turned from a piece of stock 16 inches long and ³/₄-inch square. The wands that cannot be turned can be hand-fashioned. There shall be no attempt to standardize the shape of the wand other than making it be thicker at the base and tapering the head; the wood will call out its own ultimate shape, however, the tools shall be consistent and the sandings will range from 40 grit to 220 grit dry sandpaper. Each wand will then get a light coating of Scott's Liquid Gold Wood Cleaner and Preservative to maintain the moisture of the wood and keep it from drying out. No other oils or lacquers will be applied to the wand.

The metal wands will be made in the same manner and roughly the same length, although they will probably be thinner.

In the text you will find the history of the tree, common areas it is found, characteristics specific to the tree, commercial use or value of the tree, and any myths or legends associated with the species. After that will be the reason the wood is important. Rituals and spells will be mentioned, and any magical preparation of the wand will be included, such as turning your ebony wand at the darkest hour of the new moon. There will be no popular culture references of phoenixes, unicorns, or dragons. This is a reference book of actual materials and characteristics.

Tools Make the Difference

The tools make the difference. Hand tools and power tools are both just tools of your own two hands and help you realize what you see in your mind. The tools I use on my wands today are the same tools that I grew up using. I like the Rikon 70-100 12x16-inch mini-lathe. My shop is very small, just half of a two-car garage, so I must condense everything. Also, if you try to turn anything the size of a wand in a tool much longer than 16 inches, it will bow in the middle and you will get bounce and wobble. As it is, the softer woods bounce now, so I have to be extremely cautious not to gouge or snap them.

I had a bench-mounted belt sander for a short time, but it kept burning out. I may have had a bad batch of them from the store, but in any event I went back to my standby. I have a Craftsman belt sander that I flip upside down and put in a vise on my bench. Therefore I have a portable belt sander. My drill press is bench-mounted, as are my chop saw, band saw, and jointer. When I have to mill my wood from rough cut or when I mill tree pieces, I have a table saw, and if I need to plane anything, I mount my 13-inch planer on that.

Unlike my larger power tools, which are ten years old or newer, my hand power tools have been with me for twenty-five-plus years. I have two Craftsman $^3/_8$-inch variable speed drills that I've had forever (well, it seems that way). Many of my hand planes and other small tools were from my father and grandfather, so they have been in one family over seventy-five years, either handed down or bought new for less than you can get something discounted now.

Respect Your Source Material

I try very hard not to cut a tree. I will take cuttings from tree trimmers when I know where the wood has come from, and we have some amazing people on the campus of Clemson who always keep me in mind when they trim trees. I also acquire many of my woods from specialty wood suppliers that go out of their way to avoid protected or endangered woods. However, there are times when a tree must be trimmed personally. At that time I look carefully at the tree. I speak to the tree, explain what I am looking for, and why I want it (to teach others about the magnificence of the tree), and then I feel each branch that might be eventually damaging to the growth of the tree and might need to be trimmed.

I have been fortunate that many of the trees on the periphery of the golf course I play regularly are in dire need of trimming. The owner has given me permission to trim them as I see fit, so I usually golf with clippers and duct tape in my bag for trimming and marking genus and species. It's always amusing to disappear into the woods or wander off the fairway and return a few minutes later with a tree limb sticking out of my golf bag. Those who don't know me always ask what in the world I'm doing, so that gives me a chance to talk about trees and my particular religion and life path. Most accept it, and those who don't have never said anything.

I was in Mazatlán playing golf over Thanksgiving and saw a tree that had been cut by the fairway. I had my playing partner, a Mexican businessman, stop the cart and I jumped out and ran over to the pile. I looked at the leaves, the bark, and then back to the leaves. Grabbing a piece about eighteen inches long and two inches in diameter, I threw it in my golf cart, and we played on. Eventually, my playing partner asked what I was doing, and I said I work with wood. He pronounced the wood in Spanish and I in English, and we agreed it was an example of mountain laurel probably planted as a specimen tree by the course's past owners. I declared it through customs and brought it back to work with. As I said, I pick up wood wherever I go.

The most interesting conversation I had was with a woman about my own age that I met playing golf one day. It was the day I was harvesting poison ivy vines for wands. I mentioned I would play ahead on the sixth hole and meet her on the seventh tee. At the tee I came out of the woods dressed in latex gloves, latex sleeves, and a face mask, and carrying a plastic trash bag. We had a wonderful conversation for the next eleven holes on what the heck you do with a poison ivy wand and why anyone would want one.

Deciduous Trees

Deciduous trees are those that lose or drop their leaves during some time in the calendar year. In cold climates in the fall, the trees are ablaze with the colors of oaks and maples as the leaves turn and then fall to the ground to eventually create mulch. The trees are shutting down for the winter and going into hibernation. In arid or hot climates, the leaves of deciduous trees fall to conserve moisture. For either extreme, the leaves fall and the tree goes dormant. As we will see later in the Broadleaf Evergreens section, not all leafy plants or trees are deciduous. Many of the broadleaf evergreen trees and shrubs such as holly or magnolia retain their leaves year-round.

It's interesting to note that the word *deciduous* does not just apply to trees or leafy shrubs. Baby teeth, as we are so fond of calling our first set, are referred to as deciduous teeth. Also, some deer and other antlered animals have deciduous horns that they drop before their adult horns come through.

The majority of the deciduous varieties also coincide with woods that are considered "hard." The hardwoods such as oak, maple, and the birches are sought out for furniture and other trim and specialty projects. In contrast to the evergreen trees, which are considered softwood and are used for framing houses and other construction projects, the hardwoods are slower growing, with tighter grains and cleaner lines. The harder woods conduct energy well because of their tight grain and density. However, the lighter cone-bearing woods conduct energy well because of their amount of pitch and the energy of that substance. Therefore, to think of one group of trees as being superior to another would be to do a disservice to both groups. As we shall see, each tree has its own unique characteristic and place in your repertoire.

Acacia

ORDER: *Fabales*

FAMILY: *Fabaceae*

GENUS: *Mimosoideae*

SPECIES: *acacia*

JANKA: 1750

ENERGY: Masculine

ELEMENT: Air

GOD(S) REPRESENTED: Ishtar, Osiris, Ra

GODDESS(ES) REPRESENTED: Astarte, Diana

Acacia, also called the shittah tree, is an ancient tree with historic roots going back to pre-Christian times. The acacia is identified by its distinctive thorns on the branches and trunk as well as leaves that are similar to the mimosa, a tree most are familiar with.

Uses of the acacia are varied. The gum of the tree yields gum arabic, which is used in chemicals and medicines as well as in a binding agent used in the printing industry. The seedpods of the acacia produce a seed about the size of a quarter that is either cooked or served raw, oftentimes with guacamole in Mexico. The acacia is also used as a flavoring in many international soft drinks. Medicinally the tree has been used as a tincture to cure rabies, and the tannins of the tree are used in the tanning industry as well as in many chemical components of the current age.

Historically the acacia is one of the symbols of the ancient order of Freemasons for its purity and connection to the architects of King Solomon's Temple. The tree is also associated with the tree of life in Egyptian myth, and rituals of that time used the bark and resin for mind-altering incenses, although other ingredients lost in time were also probably added. Many biblical scholars believe the burning bush was the acacia, and supposedly the one true Ark of the Covenant was constructed of acacia.

Magically a wand of acacia will give its user great power over thirst and water usage. The wand draws its magical powers from the heart of the tree and the roots that penetrate deep into the earth in search of water. Therefore, this is an excellent wand for water dowsing. Another use for the wand is historic research. The wood of the acacia has a long memory, and the genetics of the tree from seed to tree to seed to tree go back as far as before the pharaohs. Egyptian magic is another area where this wand is very powerful, and those using the acacia wand to derive powers from the Gods of Egypt and the Fertile Crescent will have greater success than any others.

Alder

ORDER: *Fagales*

FAMILY: *Betulaceae*

GENUS: *Alnus*

SPECIES: *rubra*

JANKA: 590

ENERGY: Feminine

ELEMENT(S): Air, Fire, and Water

CELTIC OGHAM: Fern

GOD(S) REPRESENTED: Bran

GODDESS(ES) REPRESENTED: Freya

The alder is a smaller tree, almost at times falling into the shrub category that is found throughout most of the northern temperate zones. In North America your best chance is to find a red alder. Interestingly enough, the alder is also a very important product of not only wood but survival. The catkins, the downy part of the tree flower, although not tasty, will keep a lost hiker fed if necessary. Also, the bark may be used as an anti-inflammatory, similar to white willow, and the wood is used for smoking seafood and fish.

Alder wood is used for guitars, and Fender has sought it out for the necks and bodies of many guitars and basses. The wood is easy to work but hard enough to give a good polish with fine sandpaper. Unlike guitars, alder wands are not coated in polyurethane or other paints, but still come out often feeling as though they have a clear coat on them.

Magically alder has many uses. Since it is resistant to water and is found near many marshy stream- and riverbeds, the wands are useful for water rituals, such as drying out after floods and heavy rains. It is also very fire-resistant and may be used to protect against fires, although other proper precautions should always be used, and a wand of alder will assist you in rituals that involve large fires. The alder has been used for centuries as a charcoal for the filtering process of some liquors, and brewers may use the alder wand in their circle prior to beginning a vintning or brewing project. Also, cooks may use the alder wand during feast preparation if they are using alder charcoal as a heat or cooking source.

Apple

ORDER: *Rosales*

FAMILY: *Rosaceae*

GENUS: *Malus*

SPECIES: *domestica*

JANKA: 1730

ENERGY: Feminine

ELEMENT(S): Air, Water

CELTIC OGHAM: Quert

GOD(S) REPRESENTED: Zeus

GODDESS(ES) REPRESENTED: Diana

I have always found it interesting that the apple is in the rose family. I have also found it interesting that the rose is actually a tree and not a shrub or a bush, even though rosebushes are sold as such. I guess all things in nature have an interesting place in science, and at times the other way around.

The apple is of both modern and prehistoric importance. The tree may be found in almost all climates and in most yards, fields, woods, and gardens. Because its seeds are easily transported and the tree survives in diverse climates and soils, it is not surprising that the cultivars and natural varieties have spread throughout the world. As a cash crop it is a staple in all levels of agriculture, from multinational companies to mom-and-pop fruit stands.

Turning apple wood is done more as a hand process. If you are lucky enough to find a large piece of apple wood, then a lathe is a good starting point, but the wood is soft, as many fruit trees are, and unless it is extremely dry the wand blank will bounce. This sounds technical, but it really isn't. The bounce is similar to a jump rope. The softer or thinner the wood, the more it will start to bow. At some point it will snap, since it cannot maintain its structural integrity. Therefore, as for many of wands in this book, I recommend you take down the rough edges with a chisel and then work the shaping and forming with sandpaper. You and the wand will both be much happier with the results.

Mythologically, there are a number of prominent legends and stories revolving around apples. The most critical to Christians is the story of the apple, Eve, and the serpent. In fact, a pomegranate was possibly the fruit originally told of in the biblical story, but the apple will forever be tied to the deception of Eve and the snake. Another story involving the apple is of Hercules from Greek mythology picking three golden apples from the Garden of the Hesperides as part of his twelve labors in repentance for a slaying. Finally, in the Norse legends apples were said to give the Gods eternal youth and vigor.

Magically the apple wand may protect against deception if it is held at the head of the wand; to assist in deceiving someone, hold the wand at the base. Crushed apple seeds have a trace amount of hydrogen cyanide, an extremely poisonous liquid. Eating apple seeds casually from time to time should not affect you too severely; however, there have been reports of people dying from eating the seeds over years and decades and building up a toxic level in their system. Whether these stories are true or not would depend on how brave, or foolish, you feel when eating apple seeds.

Apples are also good for love rituals and spells. A wand of apple will assist its user in gaining the affection of the one sought; whether it is by deception or magic is up to the user.

Following is a simple love spell to use with apple. Take an apple and cut it into four pieces, removing the seeds and seedpods. Place a quarter of the apple at each quarter of your circle, starting with the east. As you bury the apple in a shallow hole, repeat this charm:

This quarter is not a whole.
This hole is but a quarter.
My love shall come to me and I shall be one with (her/him).

When finished with the fourth quarter, use your wand to close the circle and then say this charm:

My love exists.
I shall find my love and my love shall find me.
I release my search to the Void.
Open the circle and be open for love to come your way.

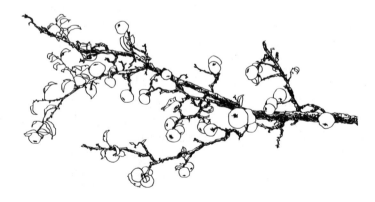

Ash

ORDER: *Lamiales*

FAMILY: *Oleaceae*

GENUS: *Fraxinus*

SPECIES: *americana*

JANKA: 1320

ENERGY: Masculine

ELEMENTS: Earth, Air, Fire, Water

CELTIC OGHAM: Nion

GOD(S) REPRESENTED: Odin

GODDESS(ES) REPRESENTED: Frigg and Minerva

The American ash, or white ash, as it is sometimes called, is one of sixty-plus species of ash that populate this continent and Europe. In fact, South America is one of the few places, other than Antarctica, where ash is not found in one form or another. A member of the olive family, the ash is a moderately hard hardwood with clear white wood and good grain. The trees are used in a number of ways, among them for the necks of guitars and baseball bats. Early airplanes were framed in ash due to its resilience and supple strength, and the Morgan Car Company in England still makes a car framed in ash.

When you are working with ash, it has a tendency to bounce on the lathe and will gouge quickly if you are not careful—and sometimes even if you are. However, if you can get past the shaping stage, the wood takes sandpaper well and needs little else.

In Norse mythology, the world tree Yggdrasil is said to be an ash, which would mean that the ash is the most important tree there is, Yggdrasil having its roots in Niflheim and its leaves and higher branches in Asgard. Yggdrasil is supported by three great roots that spring from three great wells. The first well is in Asgard and is Urd's Well; the second is in Jotunheim, where the frost giants live, and is Mimir's Well; and the third is in Niflheim at the well called Hvergelmir. The ash is related to Odin in Norse mythology and Minerva in Greek mythology. The word *ash* is the third ogham in Celtic and represents the third month of the year, March.

Magically ash is quite powerful. Both druid and witch wands have been made from ash for hundreds of years. In medieval times the brooms of witches, and others who needed brooms, were made of ash due to its strength and suppleness. The wood represents strength and prosperity. There is a ritual that places the bark of the green ash as a garter on a magician's leg to protect him or her against other magicians and their spells.

Wands of ash may be very useful for directing lightning, since ash trees attract that energy regularly during storms. If you wish to direct or collect the energy of a lightning storm, first ground yourself. This is very important. Use an ash wand and direct the energy of the lightning bolts either into your wand or away from you. If you wish to collect large amounts of energy safely, wait for a heat lightning storm and collect the static energy that way.

A side note on lightning: Magically, as atmospherically, there are two distinct types of lightning. Bolt lightning is the type we typically think of—the kind which accompanies thunder, destruction, and sometimes fires. It is a charge of energy built up in the atmosphere that finds a discharge point in the ground. The bolt forms at both ends, meeting in the middle and releasing with a loud clap of thunder. Bolt lightning is the only type of lightning that has thunder. The second type of lightning is cloud or heat lightning. This is when two clouds of static energy build to a discharge point. Since cloud lightning is more of a diffusion of energy than a direct line of it, there is no sudden collapse of energy and, therefore, no thunder.

For those who fear lightning (and let's face it, who shouldn't at least be a little wary of it?), suffer from astraphobia. Leaving a piece of ash outside in a lightning storm will help one to be less fearful of the energy discharge. Wearing a small piece of ash wood as a pendant, or carrying it with you during a storm, will help you protect yourself. Also, if you avoid severe storms and refrain from taking cover under tall trees or in open fields, you will do well in avoiding lightning strikes.

Irish immigrants who came to the United States often brought a piece of ash with them as a preventative to drowning. The ash wand, therefore, may be used for sea and water travel rituals if you are concerned with safety during your travels. Finally, if you adhere to Faery magic, the ash is one of the three sacred trees of your path, along with the hawthorn and the oak, both of which are discussed in this book.

Aspen/Poplar

ORDER: *Malpighiales*

FAMILY: *Salicaceae*

GENUS: *Populus*

SPECIES: *tremuloides*

JANKA: 420

ENERGY: Masculine

ELEMENT(S): Air, Water

CELTIC OGHAM (ASPEN): Edad

CELTIC OGHAM (POPLAR): Eadhadh

GOD(S)REPRESENTED: Tyr

GODDESS(ES) REPRESENTED: Hecate

The aspen is also known as the poplar. It is a genus that covers a large portion of the United States, between the aspens in the North or the more common poplars in the South. The poplars and aspens are able to survive forest fires due to the depth of their root structure, and therefore they regrow quickly to form new stands. While not large, they are adequate for furniture and buildings and have been used for such, although not heavily when given a choice of a denser wood.

The uses for aspen are enough to make this a significant wood in its own right. Wooden paddles and oars are still made of aspen due to its lightness and strength. Further, because it is somewhat resistant to fire, the flooring industry has continued to use aspen in flooring for homes and other buildings. Finally, the shoots that bud new trees are a staple for grazing animals, both wild and domestic, and therefore stands of aspen remain popular locations for hunters and cattlemen.

Although the white willow is most commonly thought of as a tree for aspirin derivatives, the aspen is another tree that contains salicin, an anti-inflammatory agent similar to aspirin. The bark, leaves, and flower buds are all good for pain relief and have been used for centuries by the Native Americans.

Aspen is a great wood to turn. It is light, but it doesn't bounce like ash. Therefore, it cuts very smoothly, and with a steady hand it gives you a well-shaped piece early in the wand-making process. Interestingly, when you are done sanding, the aspen will resist oils. I tried to coat the wand with Scott's Liquid Gold, and it was almost impervious to the oil.

The aspen, due to its lightness, was a prime choice for shields, and the Norse were particularly fond of imbuing their own energies and the energies of their Gods and Goddesses into their round shields before going into battle.

The aspen is similar to the phoenix in that it rises from the ashes. After complete destruction above ground due to fires, a stand of aspens will regrow quickly from its deep subterranean roots. It is for that reason that the aspen is chosen for fire-related rituals and recovery from fire spells and healing circles.

Aspen wands are very good in fire-related rituals, either for those who have suffered loss from a fire and must rebuild or those who are in fear of loss from a fire, such as those in the West, where sweeping forest fires are a constant threat. Further, those who do Faery work should look at the aspen or poplar wand, since the wood is excellent as a portal wand to enter that realm, through the shimmering cover of leaf and stem. Whatever the case, an aspen or poplar wand will hold up under most adverse situations and will perform well for you.

Basswood/American Linden

ORDER: *Malvales*

FAMILY: *Tiliaceae*

GENUS: *Tilia*

SPECIES: *americana*

JANKA: 1010

ENERGY: Feminine

ELEMENT(S): Air

GOD(S) REPRESENTED: Odin, Tyr

GODDESS(ES) REPRESENTED: Freya, Venus

Basswood is an American version of the linden found throughout Europe and the British Isles and is also called American linden. It is a large, straight-growing tree with a very identifiable leaf due to many jewelry makers casting the linden or basswood leaf in gold, silver, and other metals. The tree is used for medicinal products and as a pollen supply for beekeepers. Basswood is also very good when shade is required, since a mature tree will spread considerably. European lindens have been recorded at over one thousand years old throughout Germany and the former German provinces.

The name *bass* comes from the bast or inner fiber of the bark that is harvested as an alternate to wool and other weaving materials. The northern Japanese have traditionally used the fibers to make their ceremonial garb for centuries. In the rural South and West the basswood is used in musical instruments, and years ago when I refinished a zither for my father-in-law, I used a piece of basswood as both the back and front pieces. Drum shells are also made from basswood since it is a vibrate wood that carries sound well.

Basswood is a dream to turn on the lathe. It is soft enough to cut easily with a chisel but strong enough to not chip or jump from vibrations of the spinning. One interesting thing about the wood is that with most woods you can burn a ring on the item with a brass wire. Basswood, however, is almost impervious to that procedure. Instead of a clean, solid, and deep burn, the wood radiates the heat and gives almost a "ghost in the machine" look to the ring, radiating out from a dark but not pure-black ring to almost a faint gray.

Magically the wood is excellent for musical spells, similar to ebony. String and percussion spells will both work with basswood due to its tie to frets, faceplates, and drum shells. A wand of basswood will resonate to the sound of chanting and cast back that energy in the form of either positive or negative forces, depending on the spell cast. The wand is also good for love and lust spells and spells of immortality. It is not surprising that the Germans have used the linden as a symbol of their country, and some of their more notorious leaders, for hundreds of years.

Basswood is a favorite of apiaries since the flowers of the tree are heavily used for pollen by local beehives. This led to the basswood's connection with Gaia and the Earth Mother. The linden or basswood is the patron tree of the earth and those who revere it.

Beech (European)

ORDER: *Fagales*

FAMILY: *Fagaceae*

GENUS: *Fagus*

SPECIES: *sylvatica*

JANKA: 1300

ENERGY: Feminine

ELEMENT(S): Fire, Water

GOD(S) REPRESENTED: Odin, Zeus

GODDESS(ES) REPRESENTED: Cerridwen, Hel

Beech is a fast-growing wood that is clear-grained and grows to seventy plus feet. Although unstable for heavy building projects, the wood is used in many smaller projects such as some drum frames and rifle stocks when harder woods are not available. The European beech, or common beech, is used for plywood construction since it chips easily and holds well with glue.

Beech chips are also used in beer production, specifically in some forms of Budweiser, as well as some German beers, where the wood is used to dry and smoke the malts. The wood is further used as a smoking wood for German hams, as well as some sausages and cheeses. The Beech-Nut food line began with smoked hams in 1891 using the wood of the beech tree as its principal smoke source. Beech nuts are not as dry and bitter as acorns, but they are not a chosen food product for humans (though they are popular with some wild animals).

The wood is a good choice for anything burning and is a popular choice for those who heat their homes with it.

Magically the beech tree is important to brewers and vintners. Brewers will use the wood for filtering beer, and vintners may use the wood to heat their buildings as they work. A wand of beech will set the stage, so to speak, for successful brewing or smoking of meats and cheeses. Cast your circle around the entire building you are working in, and perform your duties in a positively charged atmosphere. Rituals that call upon the northern quarter of earth, where the trees are rooted and the grain is grown; the west, for the water that goes into the brew; the east, for the sun that grows and strengthens the hops and malts; and the south, for the fires that heat the water and the air of the building, are all important in the ritual.

Birch (River)

ORDER: *Fagales*

FAMILY: *Betulaceae*

GENUS: *Betula*

SPECIES: *nigra*

JANKA: 910

ENERGY: Feminine

ELEMENT(S): Water

CELTIC OGHAM: Beithe

GOD(S) REPRESENTED: Thor

GODDESS(ES) REPRESENTED: Freya

River birches are a joy of a tree, unless you are planting them. Then they become commonplace and less than enjoyable, with their leaf drops and brittle branches in the wind and ice. They are found throughout the eastern half of the United States, from New England to Florida. They are pretty, usually planted in threes, and give a pleasant break to the design with their thin pieces of bark lifting off as they mature. The wood is relatively useless as a building component since they are very heavily limbed and those limbs, unlike some of the harder deciduous trees, are weak and tender. You can find them around standing water or at the edges of swamps or fens. They are used often by designers to soak up standing water if no other type of swale or drainage seems to work. Further, since the trees grow in clumps rather than singularly with a long taproot, they are hazardous to cut or be around, and some birches are referred to as "widow-makers" because the limbs will fall and kill axmen.

As unuseable as the wood is for building, it is good for decorative purposes and excellent for lathe work. It is soft, and if you turn the wood while it is still slightly damp, the long ribbonlike cuts from the chisels will extend for many inches, giving you a nice byproduct for kindling and tinder. The wood doesn't bounce in the lathe and takes sandpaper exceptionally well. If you can find a knot in your piece you can get a very decorative marking in your wand.

Burning river birch twigs on the winter solstice will ensure a prosperous and beneficial new year. The river birch is also exceptionally well-poised to assist in water issues. If you live in an area that is prone to water damage or flooding, placing river birches around the periphery of your property may assist you in preventing serious damage. However, if you are fearful of heavy flooding you may wish to take more drastic measures, such as building levies, dams, or culverts.

Less than the white birch, the river birch is good for water safety when traveling. The birch will, when burned, assist the petitioner in reaching his or her destination safely and without incident. Wands of river birch may be carried for safety in travels over water, either in airplanes or boats or ships. Talismans of river birch may be as simple as a small piece of the discarded wood or as sympathetic as a carving of a boat or fish. When performing water rituals always begin the circle in the west, the quarter for water, and invoke the guardians of the west for protection against all threats from water or waterborne dangers.

Blackthorn

ORDER: *Rosales*

FAMILY: *Rosaceae*

GENUS: *Prunus*

SPECIES: *spinosa*

JANKA: 1000

ENERGY: Masculine

ELEMENT(S): Earth, Fire

CELTIC OGHAM: Straif

GOD(S) REPRESENTED: Bel

GODDESS(ES) REPRESENTED: Brigid

Blackthorn may be used as a protective shrub or small tree. The nasty thorns of the shrub are similar to the *Pyracantha coccinea* (also called the Firethorn), in that they make a very effective boundary against uninvited "guests," either the two-footed or large four-footed variety. The hedges are found throughout the countryside in northern England and northern Europe, and many have now become briar patches due to extensive migration and neglect.

The shrub is referred to as sloe, and the sloe gin so popular in the sloe gin fizz made by Old Mr. Boston and other distillers is a product of the heavy fruits of the plant. Other uses for the fruit include jams, jellies, and flavorings. The leaves are very good for tea and have been used as such for some centuries.

Irish military officers have carried "swagger sticks" of blackthorn for decades as a symbol of their rank and country of origin. Further, there is evidence that the fruit has been consumed for over five thousand years, as found in the stomachs of ancient humans found in Europe.

Surprisingly, for all the good the fruit does along with the leaves, the tree itself is associated with bad luck and negative changes in life. The Celts gave the tree the letter *Straif,* which means "strife," and therefore possibly condemned the tree to a life of toil and suffering. However, where there is strife there is renewal. After a hard frost the fruit of the blackthorn is at its sweetest, similar to frost grapes now so popular in high-end wines.

Magically the tree produces an exceptional wand for re-energization and reconstruction. A wand of blackthorn will give its wielder the power to turn his or her hard times around and find the good in the bad, thus reinventing him- or herself for a better tomorrow. The wand is also good for protection, since the thorns are physically costly to push through. If you are casting a spell for harm or strife unto another, the thorns are good "pins" to use on your poppets.

For an excellent explanation of poppets I recommend Dorothy Morrison's book, *Utterly Wicked: Curses, Hexes & Other Unsavory Notions.* With permission from the author I offer a sample here:

> The roots of the poppet, in fact, go all the way back to the ancient
> Egyptians. Instead of being made of cloth, wood, and plant materials,

though, the figure was cast of wax and designed to closely resemble the subject in question. (p. 18)

Finally, the wand is good for military or fighting spells. The Irish shillelaghs, or short walking clubs, as some have called them, were made from blackthorn, and the hard, rough surface is exceptional for "knockabout" fights. This martial spirit translates into the wand and brings its user the power to overwhelm his or her opponent quickly and decisively.

Bloodwood/Satine

ORDER: *Rosales*

FAMILY: *Moraceae*

GENUS: *Brosimum*

SPECIES: *paraense*

JANKA: 3635

ENERGY: Feminine

ELEMENT(S): Fire

GOD(S) REPRESENTED: Inti

GODDESS(ES) REPRESENTED: Mama Allpa

Bloodwood, or, as it is more popularly called now, satine, is a member of the mulberry family and is related to the fig, although the similarities stop there. Where fig is a light-colored softwood, bloodwood is a hard, tight-grained, and very dense hardwood that is tough on your tools and tougher on your sandpaper. The wood is well-priced and not on any endangered lists, making it a wonderful wood for wands and other magical instruments. When turning bloodwood, it is important to keep your tools sharpened at all times and to check them regularly, as the denseness of the wood will dull your chisels quickly. When sanding, make certain to wear a protective dust mask since the wood dust may cause nausea or excessive thirst as it dries out your throat and airways—both good things to remember when performing spells as well.

Since bloodwood/satine is related to the mulberry, the wood is very good for strength and protection spells. Its blood-red color aids the user in realizing his or her inner powers and helping to channel them through the dense wood. Also, due to its color and energy, bloodwood/satine is excellent for menstrual work, either as a maiden beginning her cycle or as a crone entering menopause. If you need cardiovascular protection, bloodwood is the perfect wood for that. Ironically, the wand is finally good for dieters, since blood moving faster in the veins is often associated with weight loss.

Canarywood

ORDER: *Fabales*

FAMILY: *Fabaceae*

GENUS: *Centrolobium*

SPECIES: *paraense*

JANKA: 1340

ENERGY: Masculine

ELEMENT(S): Water

GOD(S) REPRESENTED: Mboi Tui

GODDESS(ES) REPRESENTED: Yande Yari

Canarywood is a Central and South American wood that grows to well over one hundred feet tall and may be found throughout Panama and as far south as Brazil. It is a wonderful wood for color, oftentimes starting out as a light or medium yellow and working its way through the oranges and at times into the dark reds and browns. Canarywood is resistant to termites and other borers and is used in areas where we would normally use pressure-treated or cedar lumber.

Uses for the wood vary from railroad crossties to speaker cabinets to flooring. The wood is moderately hard, and as a tooling wood it takes chisels well and will sand to a very fine gloss. Further, the wood may be found in many marinas in flooring and on the sides of boats. It has a distinctive odor that may be unpleasant to some, but that passes quickly as the wood is sanded and then either oiled or allowed to air-dry.

Magically the wood is good for water travel and is a must for avid boaters. Musicians may also use this wood in their wands for success in the endeavors, especially if they use electronic-acoustic equipment such as electric pianos, guitars, and other stringed instruments. Singers who perform onstage may use this wood in their wands for protection against throat or other injuries prior to, during, or after performances.

If you wish to assist in the ruin of a business or person, you may use canarywood for your spell or ritual. Hold the head of the wand and cast with the base, thus reversing the resistance to termite or borer attack. This will turn the metaphoric/magical borers onto those you wish to bring down. It will also assist in the decay of whom or what you wish to damage. Saying a simple spell such as the following should yield results:

> I send out to those who would cause destruction or decay this energy to reverse your actions upon yourself.

In this way you are turning someone or something's own destruction back upon him/her/it and avoiding equal or greater damage to yourself.

Cherry (Wild)

ORDER: *Rosales*

FAMILY: *Rosaceae*

GENUS: *Amygdaloideae*

SPECIES: *prunus*

JANKA: 995

ENERGY: Feminine

ELEMENT(S): Fire, Water

GOD(S) REPRESENTED: Thor, Mars

GODDESS(ES) REPRESENTED: Artemis, The Morrigan

The species *Prunus* also includes the almond, apricot, peach, and plum varieties, which have many similarities to the wild cherry tree. They are all referred to as stone fruits because a hard pit is in the center of a softer fruit. It is interesting to note that many of these species are cyanogenic, meaning they produce trace amounts of hydrogen cyanide when crushed and then exposed to air during decomposition. Therefore, consumption of the pits is not recommended.

Wild cherry wood can be a light tan to a darker red. Furniture makers have prized cherry for centuries as a robust wood that wears well and looks good under a coat of wax or shellac. Flooring manufacturers also use wild cherry and Brazilian cherry (or what is labeled as Brazilian cherry), as they are highly sought after as higher-end wooden flooring pieces.

Many Japanese myths surround cherries, and in Japan they represent beauty, courtesy, and modesty. In China, households place dried branches of cherry over their doorways to keep out evil spirits and bad luck. In the Czech Republic, cutting cherry branches on the feast of St. Barbara is thought to enhance the Christmas holiday. St. Barbara is the patron saint of the artillery, and she protects artillerymen and -women against lighting and explosion. Therefore, the cherry branches are believed to protect the houses of those with them against winter fires or lightning strikes.

Cherry turns well and is a pleasant wood to work with. It shaves evenly with sharp tools and sands quickly. Even though it is a semihard wood, it still falls in the lower third of the Janka scale and will feel softer at times, depending on the moisture still left in it after drying. Cherry will harden and deepen in color as it ages, so turning a young or still-moist wand will be easier than a harder and more aged one. However, it is important to remember that any moisture in a piece of wood can allow it to warp once it's been turned. Therefore, you must balance the chance of warping if you turn your wand too early with the chance of splitting if you turn your wand too late.

Love spells work very well with cherry wands. Cherry wands become a deep red (well, most of them), and they represent desire as well as deep love. When initially charging your wand, you might want to also rub some cherry juice from the berries on the wood to supercharge the tool. This has a double effect of keeping the wood moist and adding the benefits of the juice. Love spells may be performed at any time, but the full moon is an excellent night for all love spells. The force of the moon, both historically and astrologically, has a strong effect on the heart and romantic issues. A cherry wand will accentuate those feelings for the user.

Another use for a cherry wand is said to be immortality. Use the wand at the darkest moon of the year. Cast your circle using the wand, and then carefully sprinkle cherry pits around the perimeter of the circle. Entreat your Deity for long life or, if you really desire, eternal life (although that does come with a price of boredom, disappointment, and commonness), and then close the circle. Once you close the circle, make certain you've retrieved all the cherry pits. Keep them safe, and it's said that as long as you have the pits you will live a long and fruitful life.

As a black belt in Kodokan judo, I know the cherry blossom has always been the symbol of our sport. However, that symbol goes back even further than 1882, when Dr. Jigoro Kano transformed jujitsu into Judo the Gentle Way. The cherry blossom has been associated with the Japanese spirit and will to win for centuries. During the Second World War the pilots who sacrificed themselves by crashing their planes and ships into the enemy vessels were known as *kamikaze*, which translates to "the divine wind," a reference to the winds that destroyed the invading Mongol fleet in Hakata Bay. Therefore, the cherry wand is very important in any sports rituals, but it is especially important to those sports that originated in Japan, such as judo, karate, iaido, kendo, and others, as well as gentler hobbies, such as sumi-e and bonsai.

Chestnut (American)

ORDER: *Fagales*

FAMILY: *Fagaceae*

GENUS: *Castanea*

SPECIES: *dentata*

JANKA: 540

ENERGY: Masculine

ELEMENT(S): Air, Fire, Water

GOD(S) REPRESENTED: Zeus

GODDESS(ES) REPRESENTED: Artemis, Diana

"Under a spreading chestnut tree / The village smithy stands." These are the first lines of Henry Wadsworth Longfellow's poem "The Village Blacksmith." Even in the early 1800s the American literary community understood the power and majesty of the chestnut tree. The chestnut is more than just a tree for poems. The nuts of the tree have been a major source of protein and other nutrients to animals and humans alike since the first nuts were discovered before the time of the kings. The Bible mentions the chestnut twice in the Old Testament.

Chestnuts are often roasted and used as a flavoring for stuffings and other internals when cooking fowl or small game. The nuts may also be dried and ground into flour for baking purposes and as a thickener for stews and soup stock. Whatever you may use the nut for, raw chestnuts will be rather bitter, so take that into consideration when planning your uses.

Magically the chestnut is revered as a tree of intelligence. Teachers and other researchers find the tree useful as a muse, and the spirits of the tree will guide the seeker to ever-greater destinies. In the Celtic tradition, the chestnut represents opportunity, and that may give you an idea of how to use the wand when you turn one. Chestnut wood is also still used for fencing posts; therefore, similar to osage orange, the wand may be used to keep things or people either in or out of specific situations or locales.

When turning a wand of chestnut, be appreciative of the nuances of the wood and the way those grains and swirls correspond to your search for knowledge and guidance. In many woods you may use either the upward or downward growth pattern as part of your design of turning, but the chestnut should be specifically turned so that any connected rings peak at the head of the wand for maximum strength.

Visioning is also very successful when using a chestnut wand as your guide. Pierce the veil with the head of the wand and, holding tightly to the base, view what is beyond. You will gain great insight into your questions if you do this in a dimly lit room with only a brown candle burning. Clear your mind of all thoughts except your question and see where the wand points you to. Similar to the wand choosing the witch, a chestnut wand will also choose the path of your direction—so let it. Don't fight the wand. The wand will always win.

Cottonwood

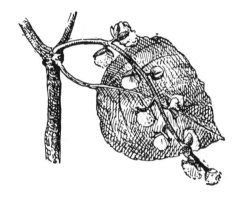

ORDER: *Malpighiales*

FAMILY: *Salicaceae*

GENUS: *Populus*

SPECIES: *aigeiros*

JANKA: 377

ENERGY: Masculine

ELEMENT(S): Air, Water

GOD(S) REPRESENTED: Tyr

GODDESS(ES) REPRESENTED: Hecate

Nothing says safety hazard like a cottonwood. The tree is wonderful for its rapid growth and wide canopy; however, the root structure is unable to support the massive size of the trunk and limbs and becomes a destructive force during high winds or storms. In some areas it's even illegal to plant the trees because of the damage they inflict on homes and businesses during excessive weather. The delicate nature of these trees to remain upright during inclement weather is not the only reason they're an annoyance. The wispy seed tails of the cottonwood, like those of the mimosa, can be a hazard to seeing and breathing. The seeds can also clog filters, which quickly causes equipment to overheat, oftentimes causing fires and blown circuits.

A wand of cottonwood, if you can get the wood to dry sufficiently to work it, has a tendency to rot quickly, so a cottonwood wand may only be a temporary one. However, temporary is relative, since it may take a generation or two before the wood becomes unable to sustain a magical energy.

Cottonwoods are much better for offensive spells than defensive ones. The wands of cottonwood will cause untold damage to others in the form of storm destruction and will act as a superior wand for airborne annoyances such as dust, pollen, and other things that may cause breathing irregularities. If you burn a smoky brazier in a circle and use a cottonwood wand, you will be able to send a disturbing amount of damage to another's lungs or eyes. The counter to a cottonwood spell of this sort would be the aspen, a cousin of the cottonwood.

Crepe Myrtle

ORDER: *Myrtales*

FAMILY: *Lythraceae*

GENUS: *Lagerstroemia*

SPECIES: *indica*

JANKA: 1055

ENERGY: Masculine

ELEMENT(S): Air

GOD(S) REPRESENTED: Rudra

GODDESS(ES) REPRESENTED: Artemis, Hathor, Aphrodite, Astarte

When I lived in Oklahoma, the crepe myrtle was a small shrub due to the aridness of the climate and the poor quality of the soil. When I moved to South Carolina, with its more temperate climate and plentiful rain, I was excited to see the trees as actual trees, some over fifty feet tall with trunks twelve inches across. The tree is a popular callout in a number of designs, and the red or white flowers add splashes of color to any drab or plain landscape.

The wood is quite tight. When I made a set of computer speaker cabinets, I was surprised to find some of the cut pieces resembled white oak. Coupled with actual red oak, the contrast is quite pleasing. On a lathe the wood cuts very well and is not too chippy or brittle. The wood is very prone to warpage, though, so make certain that the piece you are turning is completely dried or that you have the ability to steam the wand back to straight or some semblance of straight once it warps.

Magically there is little the crepe myrtle is specifically designed for. The only recommendation that I would give for this wand is to use it for escape rituals. The bark of the crepe myrtle sheds like a snake, and the underskin of the tree is so smooth that much of what comes in contact with it will slip off. I would not say it is a Teflon texture, but it's slippery enough to be referred to as monkey slip by the Japanese for its ability to repel monkeys climbing the larger specimens. The wand is good for politicians since it gives its user the ability to avoid blame or responsibility when used properly.

Cast a repelling circle with your crepe myrtle wand and cast back anything that is attempting to grasp you or bring you down or out. Holding the base end of the wand, and with a sweeping motion of your wand arm, thrust the head outward and away from where you want to be safe. While performing that motion, say what you wish to push away or repel, and for how long. Remember to be careful not to name specific people in your spell.

Cumaru

ORDER: *Fabales*

FAMILY: *Fabaceae*

GENUS: *Dipteryx*

SPECIES: *odorata*

JANKA: 3540

ENERGY: Feminine

ELEMENT(S): Water

GOD(S) REPRESENTED: Patecatl

GODDESS(ES) REPRESENTED: Venus

Cumaru is a pretty wood to work, but is also a very hard and somewhat heavy wood. The tree is native to Central America and northern South America. It is used for flooring and other purposes, but the primary product of the tree is the seeds, called tonka beans. After soaking for about twenty-four hours, the beans release an oil containing the sweet-smelling coumarin.

Coumarin is an anticoagulant that may cause hemorrhaging if taken internally, and the beans are regulated heavily by the US Food and Drug Administration (FDA). These beans, however, form the basis for the life-saving drug named above and its introduction to surgery as a blood thinner. Therefore the wood is safe to handle in tree form, but the seeds should be handled with care if you have the opportunity to come in contact with them.

Cumaru is used magically for healing and rituals to make certain a recipient survives surgery. A circle cast with a cumaru wand will give the patient added power to stave off blood clots and other circulation issues. Further, any use of a cumaru wand will assist the user in circulatory problems, when used with regularly scheduled and prescribed medical attention. Finally, if you hold the head of the wand and cast with the base, it will assist in the control of nosebleeds, although practice will be required in this one. The base of a cumaru wand is a tricky thing to control.

Dogwood

ORDER: *Cornales*

FAMILY: *Cornaceae*

GENUS: *Cornus*

SPECIES: *alba*

JANKA: 2150

ENERGY: Masculine

ELEMENT: Fire

GODS REPRESENTED: Cronus, Saturn

GODDESS REPRESENTED: Gaia

The dogwood is another tree that has been around for millennia in both literature and legend. Chaucer mentions the tree as a whipple in his *Canterbury Tales*, and the fruit of the tree has been tied to Hecate and her black hounds. The tree is so significant in the South that Virginia has the dogwood as its state tree. More than one reference to the "Old South" uses the dogwood and the magnolia as examples of true southern charm and history.

Working with dogwood is relatively easy. The wood is a finer quality and turns well. Dogwood is a small tree, though, and many of the wands made from either the alba or white variety, or the Florida or pink variety, will need to be hand-formed. I find that the dogwood is similar to working with elder if you are using hand tools; care is needed for a fine result.

Medicinally dogwood is an amazing tree for its bark, which during many times in the past, most notably during the North's blockage of the South's ports during the Civil War, was a substitute for quinine. The bark is also used for the treatment of stomach ailments, sore muscles, and menstrual inconsistencies. Care should be taken, though, when using the bark, since an overage of the powder will cause severe nausea and gastric inflammation.

I have mentioned a few of the magical properties by way of the medicinal ones. Health is a prime use of the dogwood wand. Stomach and menstrual ailments may be healed with the use of the dogwood wand in conjunction of other potions and rituals. Further, the wood has been used as a substitute for persimmon in a number of sports-related items, such as golf club heads and some high-end tennis rackets, so sports spells will do well with a dogwood wand.

For personal travel, specifically walking or hiking, use the dogwood wand in a circle for peace, safety, protection, and success. Cast your circle with the wand, and then with the head of your wand trace on a map the route you wish to take . While you are tracing your intended path, recite

> I am going out into the world in perfect trust and perfect health. I shall return in the same manner.

You will find that your path is freer of obstacles.

Finally, there are three wands in this book that work with folk magic. One is the dogwood. The dogwood is so ingrained into southern heritage that deep, low folk magic works perfectly with a dogwood wand. This is the magic of the sharecroppers, the freed slaves, and the poor white and migrant workers who worked for others. The dogwood will reach into the past and pull forward your historic southern roots for inspection, question, and retrospection.

Ebony (Gabon)

ORDER: *Ericales*

FAMILY: *Ebenaceae*

GENUS: *Diospyros*

SPECIES: *crassiflora*

JANKA: 3220

ENERGY: Masculine (but can also be Feminine in some cases)

ELEMENT(S): Earth, Fire

GOD(S) REPRESENTED: Obatala

GODDESS(ES) REPRESENTED: Yamaya

Gabon ebony is a threatened species and therefore should be acquired and used carefully. Many of the pieces that you may find in hobby shops and wood stores labeled "Gabon" are usually some other form of ebony, such as ceylon ebony (*Diospyros ebenum*). It is important to know where your wood comes from, but all ebony is treated the same due to its similar black wood and tight grain.

Working ebony takes sharp tools and a skilled hand, but with that skill it turns very well and will sand up to an almost metallic smoothness. Because of this the wands are sought by those who use dark woods and work in the dark hours and days of the month. Historically, ebony has been used for statues and pieces of furniture as far back as the pharaohs, and currently many high-priced chess sets are made from the wood. Musically, most pegs and tuning pieces on stringed instruments, as well as bass and cello bows, are made of some form of ebony.

There are two Hindu legends about ebony, and it is interesting to note that both discuss the darkness and negative aspects of the wood, though both appear in a positive way. The first is this: After the Great Flood a family saved themselves by escaping in a gourd. In the gourd they took food, water, and wood for fire. After they emerged from the gourd to a dry land, they lit the fire and left it burning as they went exploring the new world. That firewood turned to charcoal, and a piece rooted itself and became the ebony tree.

The second legend has it that a young maiden was bitten by a poisonous snake and died soon thereafter. When her family found her she was black with death, and they buried her at the base of a tree, which eventually turned black and became the ebony tree as we know it. As you can see, both legends revolve around the darkness of nature that turns the wood, not the other way around.

Ebony is a perfect wand for dark moon or new moon rituals. Anything that requires work in the dark is possible for an ebony wand. Turning a wand at the darkest of the moon will further ensure that you have a powerful tool at your disposal. Because of the density of ebony at 1.03 specific gravity, the wood does not float and therefore is useful for spells requiring something to be sunk or submerged.

Ebony is an excellent wand for protection and defense. Spells cast at a new moon with an ebony wand give the wielder extra power in their casting, and the wand will ensure that the spell is received. All work with this wand may be performed with the standard grip and orientation of the base in your hand and the head as the working end. Cunningham says in his *Encyclopedia of Magical Herbs* that ebony wands give the user unadulterated power.

Further, ebony (and basswood) are very good woods to use for musical spells, either stringed or voice. The use of ebony on frets and bows will give a clarity to a spell and make certain that the tone and meter of an incantation is heard and understood by those specifically attuned to such things.

Elder

ORDER: *Dipsacales*

FAMILY: *Adoxaceae*

GENUS: *Sambucus*

SPECIES: *spp*

JANKA: 840

ENERGY: Feminine

ELEMENT(S): Earth, Air, Fire, Water

CELTIC OGHAM: Ruis

GOD(S) REPRESENTED: Frey, Vulcan

GODDESS(ES) REPRESENTED: Gaia, Hel, Venus

"Just saying. That's the Elder Wand. The most powerful wand in the world. With that you'd be invincible." So begins the final chapter of the most powerful wand in the Harry Potter universe, as we see in *Harry Potter and the Deathly Hallows: Part 2*. The elder wands that we create are less than invincible. True, they are amazing wands, but you won't find the Dark Lord using one to control the world. This is real magic, after all.

Elder is a difficult tree to find even though there are many out there. It is found in fields and in lightly forested areas, usually as a single or as a few in a copse. There are seldom great forests of elder trees unless they were planted specifically for a reason. The berries are black to purple-black when ripe, and they fall in massive waves on the limbs, making the berries an attractive addition to your yard or garden.

Food uses vary from as far afield as a flower oil additive in Sambuca, an Italian liqueur, to a yogurt flavoring in Germany. Many wines and syrups have been made with the berries, the most famous perhaps being the elderberry wine used by the Brewster sisters in *Arsenic and Old Lace* to kill unsuspecting older gentlemen. When dealing with the elder in any form, be aware that while cooking the berries and using them is safe, any use of the uncooked berries or other portions of the tree may release cyanide in small doses. Enough small doses and you could be quite ill or deterred in your abilities. Therefore, treat this tree with respect.

Medicinally the tree berries may be used for treating the flu or other flu-like diseases. You may also use the wine in treating rheumatism or traumatic pain. Some may say that any wine will do the same thing given enough alcohol; however, the elderberry has been shown to do the job better and more exactingly.

Magically a wand from elder wood is not difficult to craft. The smaller branches are usually filled with a soft pith that does not take well to tools, and this is the reason that tree is sought out by wind musicians since the inside of the branch clears quickly and cleanly into a pipe or tube. When using a larger piece of the trunk, it is best to take the piece from the outer wall where there is sufficient stability to hold the shape. That way the lathe will have something to grab on to and the sandpaper will be able to do its job. The wood is soft, and if you can find a solid smaller branch, it may be successfully worked by hand. I make elder wands using hand tools, and the wood takes a lovely shine with fine grit sandpaper.

The elder tree is a sacred tree to Faeries, and it is said that if you stand beneath one on a midsummer eve you may see the Faeries in their realm. Also, if you cut down an elder tree, the Faeries would take that as an insult and cause damage or harm to you and your family. In Italy the elder wood is used to chase off snakes or keep thieves away from one's home or business. Finally, in the Scandinavian countries, many sailors were said to leave a portion of their soul in an elder tree to ensure a safe return. Perhaps that's where Rowling came up with the idea of the Horcrux.

Elm

ORDER: *Rosales*

FAMILY: *Ulmaceae*

GENUS: *Ulmus*

SPECIES: *americana*

JANKA: 830

ENERGY: Feminine

ELEMENT(S): Earth, Air, Water

GOD(S) REPRESENTED: Odin, Loki, Dionysus, Hermaphrodite

GODDESS(ES) REPRESENTED: Gaia, Hel, Cerridwen, Hermaphrodite

The elm has had a hard life in the past hundred years. With the advent of Dutch elm disease in the early twentieth century, many of the majestic elms that once dotted the streets and lined the thoroughfares have gone. When I was a child I lived in Manchester, New Hampshire. The main street running the length of the city was Elm Street. I remember in the west end of the city the large elms still standing, although looking poorly at that time, and I remember years later when I returned and they were all gone. Now, there are disease-resistant strains of the trees, and the majestic elms are making a comeback; but it will be another century before they regain their status as Main Street trees.

I love working with elm. The grain is very soft for a hardwood and turns quite easily. The color is more yellow than you would think, and when sandpaper is applied, the texture takes a perfect smoothness quickly and without mishap. I have not used elm for anything larger than wands, but I have some planks in the shop that I look forward to using soon. I expect the same outstanding results, and the magical energy generated by the larger items will be as well-received as the wands.

Mythically, the elm has a varied history. It is the birth tree of the mature female. In Germanic legends, woman emerged fully matured and cognizant from the elm, with all the intelligence of the Mother Goddess. Therefore, the tree is sacred to the Germanic tribes and traditions. The tree is also tied to the underworld as the tree of Hel. It is said that the elm will make order out of chaos, which is something any God or Goddess can use. The tree is also hermaphroditic, being self-pollinating, and it is therefore sacred to Hermaphrodite, God(dess) of the genders.

Magically, the elm wand will work well when dealing with the dead, the transition from life to death, or remembering the dead. As the tree sacred to Hel, an elm wand may used to penetrate the veil to the underworld and speak with one's ancestors. An elm wand may also be used for chaos magic, specifically to rectify someone else's chaos magic. Many of us know witches who either practice or claim to practice chaos magic. Many of those are chaotic enough without the magical portion. If one of your friends (or enemies, depending on your situation) casts chaos, the elm wand will work to defend against incoming chaos by organizing the spell into manageable portions or it will bounce the spell back to the originator. If, however, you have done something and inadvertently created chaos in your own life, this wand will help correct the situation.

Whatever the case, if you are facing chaos, cast your circle with the elm wand and pay particular attention to the northern quarter, where the grounding and centering will happen. Send your grounding and organized magic out into the void and bring back order. Store that order in your wand head, and with the wand "loaded" address the chaos that surrounds or affects you. Depending on the amount of chaos, you may need to do this spell more than once, but once at a time is enough. It does no good to swing the pendulum of order too far from the center, just as it does no good to swing it too far toward chaos. Once you are centered and ordered, discharge any energy left and close the circle, thanking the north for its assistance.

Ginkgo

ORDER: *Ginkgoales*

FAMILY: *Ginkgoaceae*

GENUS: *Ginkgo*

SPECIES: *biloba*

JANKA: 750

ENERGY: Feminine

ELEMENT(S): Earth

GOD(S) REPRESENTED: Wong Tai
Sin

GODDESS(ES) REPRESENTED: Tu Di
Gong

The ginkgo is an interesting tree having very few other members of its genus or family. The tree dates back to prehistoric times and comes in both male and female sexes. Ginkgo is native to China and Japan, although it has been distributed throughout the world as a specimen tree, and you may find it in parks, gardens, and mall parking lots. Its leaves in autumn are a striking yellow, and many are planted for that reason. The ginkgo is also resistant to wind and snow damage, and with its deep root structure it holds up well in dry areas, drawing water from surrounding sources.

Most ginkgos that are either clones or are planted as males. The female of the species puts off an odor often said to smell similar to rotting flesh. This smell is important for propagation but does little for pleasantries in parks and yards. The nuts of the tree are a treat in the Eastern countries, but an overconsumption of them in children will lead to a form of toxic poisoning, so moderation is suggested. Also, the seeds and other outer coatings may lead to contact dermatitis similar to poison ivy (Latin name: *Toxicodendron radicans*), so those allergic to poison ivy should avoid working with ginkgo.

Medicinally the tree has been used for many ailments. Ginkgo is taken as a supplement for memory, and many pharmaceutical companies sell ginkgo capsules over the counter. Ginkgo has also been tied to dementia and Alzheimer's disease improvement and is an important supplement in assisting blood flow in elderly and young patients.

Magically the ginkgo wand will do well for aged spells. For those who are looking to improve their health, cognition, memory, or stave off the ravages of time, this wand will be a great help. Use the wand as a visioning tool to help sharpen your acuity to memory and recognition.

A simple ritual is to light a candle at one end of a room and sit at the other end. Holding your ginkgo wand loosely in your dominant hand, point the head to a candle resting in your lap. Concentrate on the candle and work memory problems, or remember your day from start to finish. You may also recount the most important and most unimportant aspects of your week, paying close attention to the details. This will help you control any loss of memory that may be happening or that you may perceive to be happening.

Goldenrain Tree

ORDER: *Sapindales*

FAMILY: *Sapindaceae*

GENUS: *Koelreuteria*

SPECIES: *paniculata*

JANKA: 1375

ENERGY: Feminine

ELEMENT(S): Air

GOD(S) REPRESENTED: Ame-no-Koyane

GODDESS(ES) REPRESENTED: Ame-no-Uzume,
    Hae Sik Nim

The goldenrain tree is a beautiful example of a sample tree. The lanterns that are formed by its flowers are usually either yellow or orange and look like Chinese lanterns when fully in bloom. The tree is not a tall tree, but it grows with a full spread covering a lot of area. Since the tree is tolerant to many different zones, and is aggressive in the warmer climates of the Southeast and southern Midwest, many areas of the country consider it an invasive tree and have begun restricting its plantings. Nonetheless, the damage to some areas has been done and its spread is difficult to curtail.

The goldenrain tree has medicinally been used to treat conjunctivitis and epiphora, though proper medical consultation is always recommended when using any plant for medicinal purposes. The flowers are often used as dyes, and the seeds may be roasted and eaten, although this not a common occurrence in the United States.

The raintree is a perfect tree for search and exploration. The lanterns of the tree have historically been associated with explorer's lanterns, and the tree resembles a gathering of lamps on hooks. Here is a simple ritual for the goldenrain tree: Using your wand as an explorational device, cast your circle and call out what you are looking for—it could be a person or an object. Next, search the perimeter of the circle until you see the person or item approaching. It won't be able to penetrate the circle, but it will guide you from the perimeter. If you summoned a person, through meditation you may follow him or her. If it is an object you are seeking, then the item will identify itself and the location of where it is being kept/hidden.

If you are planning a trip and don't know what is before you, use the goldenrain tree wand as a dowsing rod. With a map in front of you, allow the wand to map out the best route for your vacation or other trip. Always look at the route, though, to confirm the possibility of your intended path since wands don't always take into account the limitations of their humans.

Hackberry

ORDER: *Rosales*

FAMILY: *Cannabaceae*

GENUS: *Celtis*

SPECIES: *occidentalis*

JANKA: 880

ENERGY: Feminine

ELEMENT(S): Fire, Water

GOD(S) REPRESENTED: Kumugwe

GODDESS(ES) REPRESENTED: Ixchel

Hackberries are common in most of the southern Midwest and eastern United States. They are often planted in parks, and in Oklahoma you find them on golf courses where the geese and ducks eat the blue-black berries and then leave a purple-tinted dung everywhere, polluting many water sources and requiring extensive green and fairway maintenance. All this notwithstanding, the trees do have a purpose for animal food and some human consumption. When I lived in Lawton, Oklahoma, my daughter was about five. In the late summer she would come into the house with a purple mouth from eating the hackberries that grew in our backyard. At least I always knew she was getting organic berries.

Hackberry wood is relatively soft, similar to elm, which it is often mistaken for without the berries, and ash, but it is not used for many construction projects. Mostly the wood is used for firewood, since it grows quickly and cuts easily, and in a pinch it may be used for inexpensive furniture construction.

Its medicinal and utilitarian uses are limited. Native Americans have used hackberry bark in a potion for sore throats and the berries to regulate menses. The bark is also useful for sandals, and if you boil it you can produce a dark brown or red dye for fabrics and wools.

Magically the hackberry tree has also been referred to as the hagberry tree and was shunned and avoided during the Middle Ages due to its association with witches. The wand of a hackberry tree is good for performing spells and rituals that revolve around dyes and dying of fabric. You may also use the hackberry wand for healing rituals that involve menstruation or throat ailments.

Hawthorn (Carolina)

ORDER: *Rosales*

FAMILY: *Rosaceae*

GENUS: *Crataegus*

SPECIES: *arcana*

JANKA: 1040

ENERGY: Masculine

ELEMENT(S): Air, Fire

CLETIC OGHAM: Huath

GOD(S) REPRESENTED: Thor, Zeus, Mars

GODDESS(ES) REPRESENTED: Brigid, Frigg

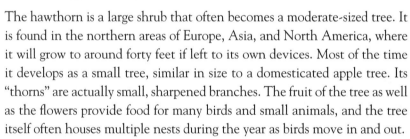

The hawthorn is a large shrub that often becomes a moderate-sized tree. It is found in the northern areas of Europe, Asia, and North America, where it will grow to around forty feet if left to its own devices. Most of the time it develops as a small tree, similar in size to a domesticated apple tree. Its "thorns" are actually small, sharpened branches. The fruit of the tree as well as the flowers provide food for many birds and small animals, and the tree itself often houses multiple nests during the year as birds move in and out.

The hawthorn has long been used as a treatment for heart conditions. The berries are used as a potion consumed for irregular heartbeats, high blood pressure, and even chest pains. The antioxidants in the berry have been shown to be effective for a number of damages to the circulatory system and may even be a deterrent to heart attacks, though the jury is still out on that one.

In Celtic legend, the hawthorn is one of the "sacred three" and is known as a Faery tree. Many families still make wreaths from the leaves and branches for the Faeries. In Arabian stories the tree has been associated with love and lust and has been claimed to increase the sexual prowess of those who eat its berries. Christian myth claims that the burning bush of Moses legend was a hawthorn, and when Joseph of Arimathea came to England his walking stick was made of hawthorn. This, it is said, is how hawthorn reached the British Isles, although the tree was probably well-established before Joseph's arrival, if arrival there was.

Hawthorns are magically effective for protection. If you cast a protection spell around your house with a hawthorn wand, you will have peace and safety. If you have cattle or other milk-producing animals and cast a productivity spell around your barn or milking area, you will get a better grade of milk and more of it.

If you make love with a hawthorn wand below you, most likely under your mattress, then you will have greater enjoyment and longevity. Point the wand toward the head of the bed and center the wand so that during the acts of sexual intimacy you are directly over it. Finally, if you use the hawthorn in a circle of contemplation, you will see the best and the worst in yourself. Use the wand carefully, though, and be of good spirits, because if you tend to see too much bad in yourself you will lose the best parts that are there too.

Hazel (American)

ORDER: *Fagales*

FAMILY: *Betulaceae*

GENUS: *Corylus*

SPECIES: *americana*

JANKA: 1470

ENERGY: Masculine

ELEMENT(S): Air

CELTIC OGHAM: Coll

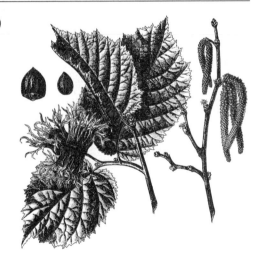

GOD(S) REPRESENTED: Mercury, Thor

GODDESS(ES) REPRESENTED: Artemis, Diana

The hazel tree has roots, figuratively and literally, in every culture across the globe. The species is found throughout all the northern climes as well as many of the southern ones, where the nuts were able to be carried by either the oceans and rivers or the birds. Being a member of the birch group, hazel wood is of little use for building, but its fruit is the hazelnut—or filbert, as it is often called.

In mythology the Celts give the hazel tree great reverence, as it is thought that the nuts, if eaten, will give its consumer wisdom and great knowledge. This comes from a Celtic myth that said nine hazel trees once grew around a sacred pond. A young druid wished for knowledge and captured one of the fish in the sacred pond. As he was cooking it, some of the hot liquid spilled onto his thumb. He sucked the thumb to ease the pain, and the wisdom was passed on to him.

Magically, other than wisdom a wand of hazel will give its user the ability to have his or her wishes granted. Cast a circle with your wand, light a small fire in the center of your circle with some hazel branches, and concentrate on your wish. Remember to be very deliberate in articulating what you wish for, but also be careful not to wish for the harm or detriment of others, human or animal. As you look past the wand into the fire, cast your wish.

The hazel wand is said to also grant its user protection from snakes and other reptiles of the earth. The wand may be used to cast a wide circle around you or around others for protection against things that slither. Remember to take precautions against poisonous snakes as well in the event that your wand is not as powerful in its resolve to assist you.

Hickory (Shagbark)

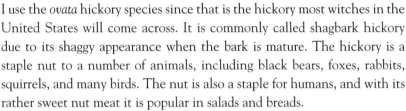

ORDER: *Fagales*

FAMILY: *Juglandaceae*

GENUS: *Carya*

SPECIES: *ovata*

JANKA: 1780

ENERGY: Masculine

ELEMENT(S): Earth, Fire

GOD(S) REPRESENTED: Apollo

GODDESS(ES) REPRESENTED: Asintmah, Mapuche

I use the *ovata* hickory species since that is the hickory most witches in the United States will come across. It is commonly called shagbark hickory due to its shaggy appearance when the bark is mature. The hickory is a staple nut to a number of animals, including black bears, foxes, rabbits, squirrels, and many birds. The nut is also a staple for humans, and with its rather sweet nut meat it is popular in salads and breads.

Hickory has been a favorite smoking wood for barbecue chefs throughout the South for over a hundred years. The bark may also be used to sweeten maple syrup that was tapped too soon and is thus too bitter or tart at the boilers.

The wood is also very heavy, and it is well-suited for furniture and handles of tools and, in older days, wagons. In the movie *Pale Rider*, Clint Eastwood's character (known simply as Preacher) declares this after he's subdued a number of ruffians with an axe handle: "[There's] nothing like a good piece of hickory."

Magically the wood is great for rituals or spells of strength. The wands of hickory will "carry" the magic to the farthest ends of the circle easily, and the energy of the wand will be clearly evident when in use. The wand is also good for healing household pets or domestic livestock.

When there is a departing spirit, the smoke from hickory is said to assist in the passing from this world to the next. The hickory wand, used in a death or passing ritual, will aid the spirit to peacefully leave this world as well as aid those who are afflicted by that spirit.

Hornbeam (Ironwood)

ORDER: *Fagales*

FAMILY: *Betulaceae*

GENUS: *Carpinus*

SPECIES: *caroliniana*

JANKA: 1780

ENERGY: Feminine

ELEMENT(S): Water

GOD(S) REPRESENTED: Sucellus

GODDESS(ES) REPRESENTED: Arduinna

American hornbeam is more commonly referred to as ironwood, and when you buy it in stores and specialty houses, you will most likely see it labeled as such. The term "ironwood" comes from the hardness of the wood and its use for handles of shovels and axes. The wood is indigenous in the northeastern United States, and there is one type of hornbeam in Europe. It is a medium-sized tree and has decorative uses as well.

The most common uses for the wood are as tool handles and cutting boards. Long-handled shovels are especially useful if made from hornbeam since the tensile strength of the wood allows the handle to be pushed to limits that would break other woods. Also, the hardness of the wood allows fine cutting boards to be manufactured since sharp knives will do little to damage the wood once it has cured and hardened.

Magically the wood is very useful for cooking spells and rituals. Because of the utility of the wood and its closeness to food production, cooks may perform rituals with a hornbeam wand and receive stellar results. Also, if you have the ability to carve out cooking tools such as spoons and forks from hornbeam and use them in lieu of a wand, the ritual and power of the spell will be doubled.

Finally, if you are building or gardening, a wand of hornbeam will be helpful for abundant crops and yields. With your wand bless your tools and seeds, then cast a circle with your wand prior to planting. Make certain that you properly thank your Deity prior to planting and at the conclusion of the harvest for favorable results next year. Also, if you use the base end of the wand to make holes for the seeds, that will result in a better and more standardized planting and a more magical harvest.

Iroko

ORDER: *Rosales*

FAMILY: *Moraceae*

GENUS: *Milicia*

SPECIES: *excelsa*

JANKA: 1260

ENERGY: Masculine

ELEMENT(S): Earth

GOD(S) REPRESENTED: Iroko (the tree is the male spirit)

GODDESS(ES) REPRESENTED: N/A

The iroko is often called African teak because of its rich grain and color. Though the tree is not related in any way to any of the teaks, many irokos are sold bearing the label "teak" to those who do not know the difference. The tree is a hardwood from the west coast of Africa and is used in boats as well as flooring and houses. The wood is very good for outside construction since, like teak, it does not require oils or varnishes to stay preserved and viable.

The tree is related to many traditions of the Yoruba people in West Africa. It is said that anyone who cuts down an iroko will be set upon by misfortune and devastation for himself and his family. The Yoruba people brought Santería to the new world when they were captured and sold as slaves. The Santería religion is a fast-growing religion in the United States and is often mistakenly classified with Voudou, although they are quite different. It is interesting that even though the tree is sacred to the Yoruba it is used in the production of djembes, a popular drum in the region.

Magically, the wood should be treated with great respect, and when a wand is acquired from this wood, the user should cast a circle immediately and thank all the Gods and spirits associated with the wand and ask for safe employment of the wand in all matters. The wand is good for water travel and percussion musical spells. Using the wand in conjunction with drums will increase the power of the ritual or spell, although care must be taken to make certain that no spirits benign or otherwise inhabit any of the drums used in the ritual.

Jatobá

ORDER: *Fabales*

FAMILY: *Fabaceae*

GENUS: *Hymenaea*

SPECIES: *courbaril*

JANKA: 2820

ENERGY: Female

ELEMENT(S): Air

GOD(S) REPRESENTED: Kurupi, Luison

GODDESS(ES) REPRESENTED: Gaia

Jatobá is found throughout Central American and northern South American forests. It is also labeled as Brazilian cherry because of its rich, deep coloration and grain. Surprisingly, it is also sometimes called South American locust even though it is neither a cherry nor a locust. This is an example of a wood being named after another species in order to make mental and visual connections easier for people.

The sap of the jatobá is a source of amber, usually referred to as "baby amber" since it is oftentimes less than 1.5 million years old, as compared to

Baltic amber, which is much older. It was probably a jatobá amber sample that was used in *Jurassic Park*.

Uses for this wood vary from flooring to furniture and other decorative items often associated with tourism. The Janka scale is high enough to keep the flooring sound for generations of regular to moderate use.

Jatobá is used in wands for generational magic, specifically ancient generational magic. The wood is aged and tied to the roots of Gaia Herself. Anyone wishing to tap into the collective spirit of the earth would use a jatobá wand and invoke the Deities of the ancient earth. Jatobá is also married to other woods, such as ebony, bloodwood, and redheart for added strength in matters of the heart, circulatory system, and divining one's past through visioning and scrying.

Leopard Wood

ORDER: *Sapindales*

FAMILY: *Rutaceae*

GENUS: *Flindersia*

SPECIES: *collina*

JANKA: 840

ENERGY: Masculine

ELEMENT(S): Earth, Air

GOD(S): Haumia-tiketike, Rongo

GODDESS(ES): Mahuika

Leopard wood is a citrus tree native to Australia, seen from New South Wales to tropical Queensland. It gets its name from the spotted bark and spots on the cross grain of the wood when it is milled. It is not a large tree compared to many of the others in this list, but is average for a citrus tree, about forty feet tall at its tallest. The tree is oftentimes found in very dry, but not arid, areas of the country where the rainfall is minimal. Further, this tree is used as a specimen tree for accent in designs, similar to how some in the eastern United States might use the river birch. Leopard wood is also a tree that does well in adverse climates and is therefore used in low-water or minimal-maintenance landscape designs.

Medicinally speaking, native cultures use leopard wood gum to make a drink, oftentimes a very sweet drink. Further, the gum is used to treat diarrhea and is therefore considered a magical herb as well as a useful tree.

Magically, wands of leopard wood are used for stomach and bowel repair and restoration. A ritual performed with a leopard wood wand has the intended recipient drinking a sweet nectar of the tree, or other citrus drinks if leopard wood gum is unavailable. The wand is then used to drive out the sickness of the stomach or intestines and restore the natural balance of the individual. The wand may also be used to cast a circle around new plantings in semiarid areas to avoid transplant shock. Fill the hole that the new plant will be placed in with water and stir that water with the leopard wood wand. This will assist the plant in assimilating to its new environment.

Lignum Vitae

ORDER: *Zygophyllales*

FAMILY: *Zygophyllaceae*

GENUS: *Bulnesia*

SPECIES: *sarmientoi*

JANKA: 4500

ENERGY: Masculine

ELEMENT(S): Earth

GOD(S) REPRESENTED: Apu

GODDESS(ES) REPRESENTED: Damara, Nantosuelta

Lignum vitae, and in this case we're focusing on the Argentine or Paraguayan lignum vitae, is sometimes also called palo santo ("holy wood") or vera. Depending on which scale you look at and whom you talk to, is either the hardest wood in the world or the second-hardest. Either way, it is not the worst wood to work with or the hardest wood to turn, in my opinion. The wood has a very attractive green tinge to the grain, and the piece I turned had a vein running through it that made one section lighter than the other, which was rather striking. Surprisingly, it's not as heavy in weight as some other woods I've worked with, so in that respect it's a pleasant wood to turn.

Depending on where you purchase your lignum, you may be buying the genus *Guaiacum*, or "true lignum," or the more common *Bulnesia*. For this book I used the more common *Bulnesia*, not wanting to chance a black market wood being added to my collection.

Uses for this wood have varied from cricket balls to ball bearings. The connecting point, though, of all the uses is that the wood is self-lubricating and useful if you are in a water setting. Many of the bearings in submarines and sailing ships were made from lignum. This self-lubricating is a problem when you are trying to sand a lignum wand. The oils in the wood clog up the grit of the sandpaper, making it almost useless quite quickly. However, that fact notwithstanding, the wood sands up very well and rather pleasantly.

The second problem with lignum is that it won't burn. The oils in the wood, even after extensive drying, will keep a wire from heating up, and all you get is an oily line where the pressure of a wire dented the wood. Third is that the wood warps very quickly. I used a 1.5 x 1.5–inch piece for four wands. By the time I cut the wood, one side had curved, making it impossible to turn it on a lathe.

The T. H. White novel *The Once and Future King* states that the wand used by Merlin in the series is made from a lignum branch and is therefore quite powerful. This is a departure from most other Merlin legends in which Merlin is said to have a wand of oak.

Magically, a lignum wand is excellent for machinists. Anyone who uses mechanical equipment for a living or a hobby should have a lignum wand. The lubrication in the wand and the history of the wood in mechanical parts will generate a strong field for success in one's endeavors. For those who enjoy the physical pleasures, there is a legend that the bark of the lignum tree is good for contraception and by extension the wand may stave off unwanted pregnancies. It should be noted, however, that I have no information to the effectiveness of that claim and would strongly recommend practicing additional and more proven methods of contraception as well.

Locust (Black)

ORDER: *Fabales*

FAMILY: *Fabaceae*

GENUS: *Robinia*

SPECIES: *pseudoacacia*

JANKA: 1700

ENERGY: Feminine

ELEMENT(S): Earth, Water

GOD(S) REPRESENTED: Amaethon

GODDESS(ES) REPRESENTED: Hecate, Cerridwen, The Morrigan

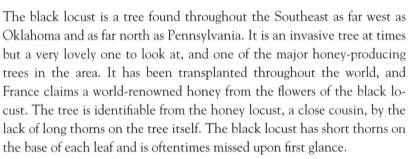

The black locust is a tree found throughout the Southeast as far west as Oklahoma and as far north as Pennsylvania. It is an invasive tree at times but a very lovely one to look at, and one of the major honey-producing trees in the area. It has been transplanted throughout the world, and France claims a world-renowned honey from the flowers of the black locust. The tree is identifiable from the honey locust, a close cousin, by the lack of long thorns on the tree itself. The black locust has short thorns on the base of each leaf and is oftentimes missed upon first glance.

Uses of the tree are many. The flowers are used in cooking but must be heated sufficiently since the leaves and flowers have caused depression, weakness, and cardiac palpitations in horses that have eaten the leaves or flowers raw.

The wood is prized for furniture makers for its density and hardness. In many farms and fields throughout the United States and Europe black locust wood is grown and used as fence posts. There is a legend that

Abraham Lincoln spent much of his youth splitting black locust wood for fence posts.

Magically the tree and wands are good for protection and strength. They are also used for binding someone's will to your own and if you so need it to cause physical enchantments. In a circle create a poppet (see Dorothy Morrison's book, *Utterly Wicked: Curses, Hexes & Other Unsavory Notions* for how to do this). With your poppet in hand, pull the will of the individual in question to you or bind his or her will to yours so that he or she will do as you desire. When you are finished with the poppet, release the spirit of the individual and bury the poppet. This will allow any residual energies to ground back to the soil. Remember, if you perform such a ritual, you are influencing the will of another and must be aware of the karmic consequences.

Mahogany

ORDER: *Sapindales*

FAMILY: *Meliaceae*

GENUS: *Khaya*

SPECIES: *spp*

JANKA: 830

ENERGY: Masculine

ELEMENT(S): Fire

GOD(S) REPRESENTED: Amadioha

GODDESS(ES) REPRESENTED: Ala

Mahogany is another wood that has a number of names, not all of them accurate. The true mahogany is native to Central and South America. However, there are other species that have taken root as far north as Florida and the Bahamas, so the trees are plentiful in a variety of species.

The wood is hard and deep in color with a tight grain. It is very useful for furniture, and veneers are seen on walls in both commercial and residential buildings. As far back as prehistoric times the indigenous peoples of Central and South America have used the trees as canoes, and in the 1500s the Church made crosses of mahogany.

However, there is another mahogany that is the true mahogany. This is the *Khaya* genus from Africa, and it is the mahogany that I use for my wands since it is not on the endangered species lists. Natives of West Africa use the leaves and shoots of this species for their cattle during the dry season, and the bark is used to treat some diseases because the seeds contain oils of palmitic, stearic, and oleic acids.

Magically wands of African mahogany are good for healing and keeping livestock healthy. Spells and rituals that use the African mahogany wand may cause increased productivity in one's cattle, with proper care and feeding, as well as health and happiness.

Wands of the Central American mahogany are good for small boat travel and success in craft and woodworking projects. Casting a circle around your work area or shop before beginning an important wood project will increase the chances of success.

Maple (Sugar)

ORDER: *Sapindales*

FAMILY: *Sapindaceae*

GENUS: *Acer*

SPECIES: *saccharum*

JANKA: 1450

ENERGY: Masculine

ELEMENT(S): Earth, Air

GOD(S) REPRESENTED: Jupiter

GODDESS(ES) REPRESENTED: Rhiannon, Venus, Athena

Maple is a very diverse and prolific tree. There are approximately 128 different species on the planet, and much of our furniture wood is maple. In the Northeast and throughout Canada, the sugar maple is tapped in the spring to make maple syrup used the world over as a sweetener and covering to pancakes and waffles. The leaves of the tree provide much of the color that is so famous in the New England fall season.

The Algonquian peoples of the northeastern United States and Canada are credited as being the first to develop maple syrup. They also made candy, which was really just crystalized maple sugar, very much like the candies we have today, by boiling sap and then placing it in the snow. The tree was so important to Native Americans that the Ojibwa had a maple god named Ininatig.

Turning the maple may be done with standard sharp tools on a lathe, and final sanding is relatively easy, producing a good, clear surface. Many pieces may be found to be of reddish color and are sought as furniture pieces and other decorative items. The color, although aesthetically pleasing, does not add nor detract from the power of the wand. The maple is an excellent carrier of sound, and many fine stringed instruments are either made entirely of maple or the necks are.

The sugar maple, also known as rock maple, is highly prized in flooring as well as in pool cues, baseball bats, and bowling pins. For this reason spells and rituals involving strength or the request for strength, to combat bodily injury or to participate in sports competitions, should be performed with a maple wand. The wand is very useful in love spells and rituals since the sweetness of the sap and the ultimate creation of the candy and syrup lend themselves to the power of love and attraction. In a love or lust spell you may use either a maple candy, eating some during the ritual, or maple syrup, again consuming some or adding it to your cakes during cakes and wine.

The seedpods of the maple look like small helicopter blades and when tossed up into the air they auto rotate to the ground. For that reason a sugar maple wand is also very good for flying spells when you either fly to travel, for enjoyment, or jump out of airplanes in the form of parachuting. The wand will assist you in a safe takeoff and even safer landing. During the ritual if you are flying use one of the double seedpods as a form of sympathetic magic; throwing it into the air and casting the spell as the pod safely flies down to the ground. Then carry that seedpod with you for added benefit. Note: This is applicable only in areas where carrying foreign plants and seeds is not prohibited.

As a final benefit to a maple wand, the tree is very useful for changing. If you need to change something or you are in the middle of changes that you may or may not be able to control, the maple wand will help cut through the clutter and get you on track.

Maple (Ambrosia)

ORDER: *Sapindales*

FAMILY: *Sapindaceae*

GENUS: *Acer*

SPECIES: *rubrum*

JANKA: 1450

ENERGY: Masculine

ELEMENT(S): Earth, Air

GOD(S) REPRESENTED: Jupiter

GODDESS(ES) REPRESENTED: Rhiannon, Venus, Athena

An ambrosia maple (also called the swamp, water, or soft maple) is actually a red maple that has been infected with the ambrosia beetle. The beetle burrows into the wood and creates a trail of ambrosia fungus, causing the wood to become streaked with a darker color. It is the coloration of the wood that builders and craftspeople seek. The wood itself is rather dry and cracks easily for a maple, so care should be taken when dealing with the wood. Usually the wood is sealed prior to shipping to keep it as moist as possible.

Magically the wood is good for artisans and craftspeople who are looking for success in visual arts more than written arts. Also, if you are bothered or "infested" with people or things and wish to be rid of them, this wand is good for clearing the clutter and removing those bothersome things in your life.

Maple (Curly)

ORDER: *Sapindales*

FAMILY: *Aceraceae*

GENUS: *Acer*

SPECIES: *saccharum*

JANKA: 1450

ENERGY: Masculine

ELEMENT(S): Earth, Air

GOD(S) REPRESENTED:
Jupiter

GODDESS(ES) REPRESENTED:
Rhiannon, Venus, Athena

The curly maple, or tiger maple as it is usually known, is found in both hard and soft maples. The curl of the grain is not evident until the tree is milled. While there is no clear reason for why the grain appears to curl, the distinctive pattern of the wood is much sought after by woodworkers. The wood is used primarily for veneers and musical instruments, especially guitars. The Les Paul line of classical guitars uses the flame maple pattern for its faces and backs. The curl in curly maple is caused by the variations of the wood fibers, making the wood attractive but also structurally unstable at times. Therefore, curly maple is not suited for large, strength-related projects.

The wood is enjoyable to turn and creates very detailed patterns in the wands, although not as detailed as in large samples such as countertops or musical instruments. It is a light wood, being a member of the maple family, and sands well, although, as with many of the softer of the hardwoods, it has a tendency to become grained and rough as the years wear on. Therefore, keeping this wand oiled is advisable.

Other historic uses of the tree include paddle wheels (You don't see too many of those around anymore do you?) and spindle wheels (Again, not in high demand.). These two historic aspects lend themselves to the magical qualities of the wood.

Curly maple is very good for weavers and spinners. The curl of the grain emulates the patterns of the yarn and the coloration of the wool, making it ideal for spells of success and profit for those of the trade. Also it is very useful for protection and success spells when one is traveling by water, whether in small crafts such as boats and canoes or large ocean liners. While we may think that ocean liners are safe to travel on, tragedies such as those that occurred on the *Titanic*, *Lusitania*, *Andrea Doria*, *Costa Concordia*, USS *Cole*, and *Achille Lauro* serve as reminders of the great loss in lives and property.

Wands made from curly maple may also be used for healing, communication, binding, and prosperity. These spells may be interchanged with the ones for the sugar maple.

Mesquite

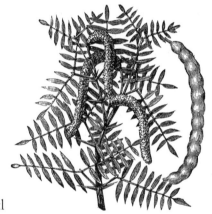

ORDER: *Fabales*

FAMILY: *Fabaceae*

GENUS: *Prosopis*

SPECIES: *spp*

JANKA: 2200

ENERGY: Feminine

ELEMENT(S): Air, Fire, Water

GOD(S) REPRESENTED: Quetzalcoatl

GODDESS(ES) REPRESENTED: Tlaltecuhtil

Mesquite is a wood that is automatically associated with a geographical region due to its use in barbecue and meat smoking in the Southeast. The tree is found in drought-prone locales where rainfall is minimal. The roots of the tree extend far into the ground to find any water available, oftentimes competing with other trees and grazing grasses for moisture. For that reason, in some areas of the world the mesquite is now a nuisance tree, and programs to eliminate them are underway.

The tree is a small one, almost a shrub in some areas, with long seed-pods. The trees during their growth phase may grow spines that reach three inches in length and thus become a secondary nuisance to children playing around them or animals that brush up against the trunk and limbs.

The wood is excessively hard after drying and will take a very sharp chisel to turn successfully as well as more labor to sand the wand. For these reasons the wood is highly sought after for some aspects of furniture manufacture. However, the grain of the wood is very attractive and therefore it is used in a number of decorative projects too.

Medically the wood is of little use anymore. At one time a local tincture was made of the bark to treat eye irritation.

The bean pods may be ground into flour and used for baking or used for jellies or a wine flavoring. The wood, though, is most prized for its smoky flavor. The wood burns very slowly and produces a lot of controlled heat for meats and potted meals. Also, the woody flavor from the smoke is highly sought after in cooking competitions.

Magically the wood is good for cooking spells. A wand made from mesquite is very useful during Wild West competitions and barbecue and chili contests. Here's a sample ritual to perform before leaving for a cook-off: First, create a circle. Next, cast a spell over your ingredients. Make certain that the mesquite wood you are using as your heat and flavoring source is also in the circle with you. Envision the trophy or prize in your hand and invoke the spirits of the wood to ensure a first-place finish. When you get to the competition, cast a semipermeable circle around your area to keep out other spells and to retain your magic in your specific area.

Mimosa

ORDER: *Fabales*

FAMILY: *Fabaceae*

GENUS: *Mimosa*

SPECIES: *spp*

JANKA: 1400

ENERGY: Feminine

ELEMENT(S): Air, Water

GOD(S) REPRESENTED:
Saturn

GODDESS(ES) REPRESENTED:
Artemis

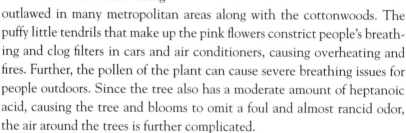

The mimosa is a beautiful specimen tree that is now being outlawed in many metropolitan areas along with the cottonwoods. The puffy little tendrils that make up the pink flowers constrict people's breathing and clog filters in cars and air conditioners, causing overheating and fires. Further, the pollen of the plant can cause severe breathing issues for people outdoors. Since the tree also has a moderate amount of heptanoic acid, causing the tree and blooms to omit a foul and almost rancid odor, the air around the trees is further complicated.

The tree, despite its drawbacks, is still wonderful to view. The gentle breezes will move the light, airy leaves and branches. and the trees seem to dance in a moderate wind. When touched, the leaves will close up quickly, reminiscent of a Venus flytrap and other movement plants. This gives the tree an almost cognitive appearance when playing around it.

The wood is very hard. When I was given a piece of mimosa to work, it was about five inches in diameter and not more than four feet tall but weighed in excess of thirty pounds. The denseness of the wood is evident when you try to turn it. The grain is more stringy, and there is a gray streak that runs along the wood as you get closer to the very dark brown and tightly grained heartwood.

An Indian myth of the mimosa is given in the *Shatapatha Brahmana*, where a human fell in love and married a wood nymph. The grounds of the cross-world marriage was that the nymph never see her husband naked. The other nymphs wanted their sister back and conspired to have the nymph view the naked husband. To regain the wife he had lost, the nymphs agreed if he would build a fire with mimosa for a year and then cook rice on that fire he could sacrifice himself to join his wife. He did so and became a *gandaharva*, which is the male version of a female wood nymph.

Medicinally frankincense is said to be produced by the mimosa (but not the one local to the United States). This frankincense is from a different species similar to the mimosa that Virgil speaks about in his writings and that Theophrastus calls an acanthus, although that may be a misnomer too.

Magically the mimosa is good for two very diverse things. As an offensive wand, the spell cast with a mimosa will cause the intended victim to suffer great boughts of coughing and prolonged breathing difficulty. A simple projection spell is all that is necessary for such calamitous results.

For a personal spell, the mimosa wand is very good for dancers and those who wish to connect with their spirit of movement. Cast a circle with the mimosa wand and then practice whatever routine you may have within the circle. The energy from the wood will carry you to new heights in your dance, gymnastics, or other movement routines. If you cast a circle around an entire gymnasium for practice, make certain that you alert and gain permission from all those who may cross your circle or be affected by the spell.

Monkey Wood

ORDER: *Fabales*

FAMILY: *Fabaceae*

GENUS: *Platymiscium*

SPECIES: *pinnatum*

JANKA: 3100

ENERGY: Feminine

ELEMENT(S): Air

GOD(S) REPRESENTED: Kokopelli

GODDESS(ES) REPRESENTED: Pachamama

The monkey wood tree is often incorrectly referred to as the monkeypod tree in local customs, and in some catalogs and stores it is listed under macacauba. Do not be misled. The two trees are not the same. Monkey wood is a wide-canopied tree with brittle branches that may cause damage during heavy storms. Though it is used extensively on the sides of roadways and walking paths, this is not advised, for it's dangerous to vehicles and pedestrians. The range of the tree is throughout Central and South America, and it may be found as far south as Venezuela. Varieties are also found in the Pacific Islands, Hawaii, and Southeast Asia. There are nineteen species of the tree, but only the *pinnatum* has opposing leaves. The tree is heavily used for furniture and construction and gives a high gloss when waxed.

Turning monkey wood is not difficult. Even though it is high on the Janka scale, it is a softer wood to work and looks very light, almost tan, when it is on the lathe. It takes sandpaper very well, and when you put a coat of Scott's Liquid Gold on the wand, it brings out an amazing pattern that makes the wood look speckled. The end grain is open and needs to be sanded down to a very fine grit, no less than 220, to take out some of the openness. When oiled, the pores close up some, and I recommend that the wand be kept oiled; however, that choice is yours.

Magically the monkey wood is a good choice for musicians. The wood is related, somewhat, to other rosewoods and is used for sides and facings of acoustic guitars. Wands of monkey wood should be used for rituals and spells about performing or increasing your productivity and creativity for lyrics or music. If possible, turn or make your wand from the same piece of wood that your guitar was made from. This in all probability is not likely, but it will give you an amazing amount of positive energy for your spell.

Mulberry (Red)

ORDER: *Rosales*

FAMILY: *Moraceae*

GENUS: *Moreae*

SPECIES: *rubra*

JANKA: 1600

ENERGY: Masculine

ELEMENT(S): Air

GOD(S) REPRESENTED: Fujin, Fei Lian

GODDESS(ES) REPRESENTED: Kichijoten, Inari Okami

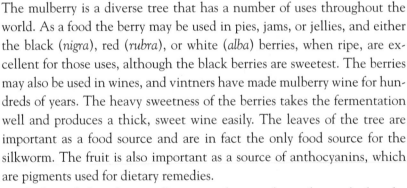

The mulberry is a diverse tree that has a number of uses throughout the world. As a food the berry may be used in pies, jams, or jellies, and either the black (*nigra*), red (*rubra*), or white (*alba*) berries, when ripe, are excellent for those uses, although the black berries are sweetest. The berries may also be used in wines, and vintners have made mulberry wine for hundreds of years. The heavy sweetness of the berries takes the fermentation well and produces a thick, sweet wine easily. The leaves of the tree are important as a food source and are in fact the only food source for the silkworm. The fruit is also important as a source of anthocyanins, which are pigments used for dietary remedies.

In legend the white mulberry was forever changed to red after the death of Pyramus and Thisbe. The two lovers were to meet under a mulberry tree, but through a series of misfortunes, including an encounter with a lion, each thought the other was killed, and in the end both killed themselves on Thisbe's sword. When the Gods saw what had happened, they turned the berries of the mulberry tree bright red to immortalize the true love of the two.

Magically the mulberry wand is used for love spells if there is conflict during a courtship or marriage. The wand will help alleviate problems and smooth the way to a fruitful union. To perform the spell, find a few berries and some dried leaves and branches of a mulberry tree. Place the mulberry pieces in a brazier and over the top place a photo or representation of the two people who are having problems. Cast a circle around your working area and then place the mulberry wand on the altar in front of the brazier. Draw or inscribe on a piece of paper the cause of the conflict, whether it be money, a person, a situation, etc. Light the piece of paper, and as you touch off the mulberry and the photo in the brazier, say

> I burn away all that stands between our love. Be gone all difficulties, and in your place create smooth and joyous pathways.

As the brazier burns, take your wand and invoke the lesser-banishing pentagram. When the wood, leaves, and paper have burned out, bury the ashes under a mulberry tree if you can find one, or a cherry tree. Your obstacles should be gone forever.

Oak

As I mentioned earlier, oak is an odd genus. There is white oak and red oak, and they are very different from one another once the bark is removed. In each category of oak there are a number of different species, and each species has a specific use. However, each category has similar uses throughout the grouping, and moving up the chain all oaks have similar characteristics across the board.

Red Oak

ORDER: *Fagales*

FAMILY: *Fagaceae*

GENUS: *Quercus*

SPECIES: *rubra*

JANKA: 1290

ENERGY: Masculine

ELEMENT(S): Air, Fire

CELTIC OGHAM: Duir

GOD(S) REPRESENTED: Cernunnos, Herne, Thor, Zeus

GODDESS(ES) REPRESENTED: Artemis, Brigid, Cerridwen, The Morrigan, Diana

Red oaks are identified by their non-rounded leaves. Even though there are many different leaf shapes and sizes, such as the blackjack oak (*Quercus marilandica*), the water oak (*Quercus nigra*), and the pin oak (*Quercus palustris*), the leaves all have non-rounded edges. It is the red oaks, and specifically the southern red oak, that is the prime oak for lumber. The trees are solid, well-grained, and depending on the age and mineral compositions of the soil, veined so heavily that the wood resembles a number of other genera.

Turning red oak is a joy since the wood is hard when dry and tends to stay put on the lathe. There is very seldom any bounce to the wood, and although it takes a lot to sand it to a perfect smoothness, when it is sanded as such it retains that polish well. Further, it takes oils extremely well, and many oils bring out the nuances of the grain that are invisible to the naked eye.

Medicinally there is little that is used in the oaks. The acorn is edible to humans, although it is dry and bitter. Animals favor the nuts, and consume them without chewing, thus dropping fertilized acorns in their scat.

Magically all oaks are strong and protective. The red oaks by species each have specific characteristics that lend themselves to a variety of uses.

Blackjack Oak

SPECIES: *marilandica*

The blackjack oak is a survivor. Where many other trees and shrubs require moist soil and nutrients, the blackjack will grow in poor and dry soil just as well as in better conditions. The wood is used for barbecue briquettes and cooks favor the wood since it burns very hot and intensely. The acorns of the blackjack, while good for deer and fowl, should be kept away from bovines due to the high concentration of tannic acid in them. Blackjack oak is easy to identify since the leaves are shaped like a club, hence the name "blackjack," derived from a favorite of highwaymen in the Middle Ages.

Magically the blackjack oak has a number of very important features. Cooks may use the wand to cast a circle around their fires and pits for safety or for success during competitions. Hunters may use the wand as a stirring instrument when preparing tanning soaks, using the natural tannic acid in the nuts as a product of the hide preparation process. For those who are pugilists, a wand of blackjack oak will assist the user in rituals for success in boxing. Make certain when performing the ritual or circle that you do not identify anyone by name or designation; merely ask for success in your sporting endeavors.

Pin Oak

SPECIES: *palustris*

The pin oak is oftentimes confused in name with the chinkapin oak (*Quercus muehlenbergii*) because people can't say chinkapin and just shorten it to pin. This is worrisome on a number of levels, since the chinkapin oak is a white oak and the pin oak is a red oak. Also, the leaves are quite different and the woods are strikingly varied from each other.

The pin oak is well-suited to water areas, although not flooded ones, and will survive to be the dominant tree in many forests since it grows quickly and wastes little on lower branches, putting all its resources into height. Further, the tree puts out a large number of acorns, thus ensuring that the tree is well-represented in the competitive new growth level of the forest.

Magically the pin oak wand may be used for pain in the stomach or intestines, and a ritual for those areas would do well with a pin oak wand since the entire genus is good for protection.

Water Oak

SPECIES: *nigra*

The water oak is an excellent source of lumber-quality wood, usually sold under the general category of red oak. The grains are long and dark, giving it the typical red tint that most of the red oaks have when cured and seasoned. The leaves of the water oak are easy to identify since they look like paddles, and the tree is found in low-lying areas where flooding and marshing occur regularly.

Magically the water oak is good for protection again flooding, especially in basements and lower levels of houses. Cast a circle around your house, and then while under protection of the ritual or circle, do repair work to the foundation or basement walls. This will assist the repairs in working the first time and lasting.

White Oak

ORDER: *Fagales*

FAMILY: *Fagaceae*

GENUS: *Quercus*

SPECIES: *alba*

JANKA: 1360

ENERGY: Masculine

ELEMENT(S): Air, Fire

CELTIC OGHAM: Duir

GOD(S) REPRESENTED: Cernunnos, Herne, Thor, Zeus

GODDESS(ES) REPRESENTED: Artemis, Brigid, Cerridwen, The Morrigan, Diana

The white oaks are softer oaks, at least as oaks go. They are used in a similar manner as the red oaks for hardwood lumber, furniture, and other general craft, hobby, and construction projects. The white oaks can be identified by their rounded leaves. The white oaks are your field-working oaks, being much more decay-resistant in water and wet conditions. Also, the acorns of the white oaks are tastier, although still not a desired meal to most.

Post Oak

SPECIES: *stellata*

The post oak is a perfect example of name following function. The small white oak is used primarily for fence posts in the fields and plains of the eastern United States. The rather small tree lends itself well to the decay-resistant straight wooden posts necessary to keep animals either in or out. Further, the post oak is a popular choice now in Texas barbecue.

Magically the wand will work exceptionally well for either keeping things in or out of a property dispute or area. When protecting yourself against trespassers a wand of post oak will do very well and respond naturally to the request. Further, for trail cooks who compete in cooking and smoking competitions, this wand, when used in a ritual of success, should lead the owner to a successful competition.

Chinkapin Oak

SPECIES: *muehlenbergii*

The chinkapin oak is the most prevalent of the thin-leaved white oaks. The wood is found throughout the Southeast and provides sweet, edible acorns. The chinkapin oak has the best-tasting acorns of all the oaks, and these can be used either raw or cooked in salads and breads.

Magically the chinkapin may be used as many other oaks for protection and strength. Traditionally, carrying a chinkapin wand while hiking will ensure that you will become neither hungry nor lost and will return safely to where you started.

Southern Live Oak

SPECIES: *virginiana*

The southern live oak is indicative of the Deep South. Songs are sung referencing the oaks, and the photos of the old oaks make up many of the backdrops of Civil War and antebellum movie sets. The live oak is an evergreen oak, which means it retains its leaves in the winter and drops its leaves only when necessary.

The wood of the live oak is some of the hardest in the oak genus. The frame of the masted ship "Old Ironsides" was constructed of live oak, and the US Navy has never sold off a large portion of its land that houses stands of southern live oak.

Magically the live oak is a wonderful wood to make a wand from if you are working with ship magic or water magic. Also, the wand will cast strong and powerful circles and rituals to keep you safe and secure against outside forces either positively misdirected or deliberately thrown at you.

Olive

ORDER: *Lamiales*

FAMILY: *Oleaceae*

GENUS: *Olea*

SPECIES: *europaea*

JANKA: 3700

ENERGY: Masculine

ELEMENT(S): Earth, Air, Fire, Water

GOD(S) REPRESENTED: Hercules, Horus,
Zeus, Ra, Apollo

GODDESS(ES) REPRESENTED: Athena,
Amaterasu, Minerva

The olive tree is a long-lived fruit tree that
is indigenous to southern Europe and the Med-
iterranean. The history of the tree dates to prebiblical times, and Noah is
said to have received an olive branch when he sent the doves off the Ark
after the great flood. Winners of the Olympic Games were given wreaths
of olive branches and awards and jars of olive oil as prizes. The oils were
highly prized in ancient times, and entire cultures grew up around orchards
and pressing plants.

Cooking with olive oil is prevalent everywhere. There are stores that
sell nothing but flavored olive oil, and EVOO (extra virgin olive oil) is
an acronym heard on many cooking shows. Olive oil is also flammable, so
lamps using the oil have existed for over four thousand years. Olives were
even found in the tomb of King Tutankhamun.

Mythologically, the oil was so important in Greece that for centuries
only virgin men and women were allowed to harvest the olives; otherwise
the fruit would be tainted. Also, in the battle for naming the new city of
Athens, the Gods granted the winner of a contest with the right to name
the city. Poseidon struck the ground and caused a spring to well up, thus
providing water for the city. Athena struck the ground and an olive tree

grew. Such was the importance of the olive that the Gods granted her the favor and named the city after her.

Magically the olive tree is linked to longevity and immortality. A wand of olive wood may be used to prolong life by drawing energy from the Aether. Also, using an olive wand in cooking rituals will yield more nutritious foods (if healthy ingredients are used), and one's health should improve.

Olivewood (Bermuda)

ORDER: *Celastrales*

FAMILY: *Celastraceae*

GENUS: *Cassine*

SPECIES: *laneana*

JANKA: N/A

ENERGY: Female

ELEMENT(S): Earth

GOD(S) REPRESENTED: Iroas

GODDESS(ES) REPRESENTED: Roma

The Bermuda olivewood is a protected wood and limited to places such as the Bermuda Botanical Gardens, where I first encountered it, and other local areas on the islands.

For those fortunate enough to have a piece of this wood, it is good for tanning and leather production. The wand will assist the leatherworker to be more productive and more successful.

Olivewood (Black Ironwood)

ORDER: *Lamiales*

FAMILY: *Oleaceae*

GENUS: *Olea*

SPECIES: *capensis*

JANKA: 3120

ENERGY: Male

ELEMENT(S): Earth

GOD(S) REPRESENTED: Denka

GODDESS(ES) REPRESENTED: Fecunditas, Feronia, Hestia

The olivewood you will most likely find in wood stores is not really olivewood, but rather black ironwood. It is a member of the olive family found in Africa and some isolated areas of the Middle East. The wood is harvested from the tree and hard and oily when dry. The grains are tight and very colorful, although the yellows and dark browns make the wood look streaked.

Turning olivewood takes sharp tools but will work well if given the chance. It is hard to find a long and straight piece of the wood, and wands are most likely made in the ten to fourteen–inch range due to the availability of material. Even sanded and dry the wood has a slight oily feel, but not enough to be unpleasant.

As a food source the fruit is very fragrant and when ripe is large and enjoyable. The olives from the tree may be used for a number of projects, and the oils are similar to any of the real olive trees.

Magically the wand is good for cooking as well as moving fire energy around. I spoke with a young witch at a conference who found that the olivewood wand works well at controlling his fire element without stress and it "felt right" in his hand. Although not every wand is for everyone, this is something to consider when looking for a southern wand for circle or ritual.

Orange

ORDER: *Sapindales*

FAMILY: *Rutaceae*

GENUS: *Citrus*

SPECIES: *sinensis*

JANKA: N/A

ENERGY: Masculine

ELEMENT(S): Fire

GOD(S) REPRESENTED: Cupid

GODDESS(ES) REPRESENTED:
  Venus

The orange is actually a hybrid between a pomelo and a mandarin and was possibly hybridized as early as 2500 BCE. During the Middle Ages orangeries were very popular in European countries that were too cold to have oranges year-round. The containers, often referred to as Versailles planters after the most famous ones of Louis XIV, were kept in orangeries during the winter and taken out in the summer. Although Charles VIII was the first to introduce oranges to the French on a large scale, Louis took orange production to new heights, having at times over a thousand trees at once.

While there are many species of oranges, the most common ones are those you see in the grocery stores, such as the Valencia. After a disease-ridden year in Florida, most of the orange trees were forcibly cut down to prevent spreading, and there are few orange trees left in the southern section of the state. However, oranges are still flourishing in northern Florida and throughout the South from one coast to the other.

Medically, oranges, like all other citrus fruits, were popular for preventing scurvy in sailors and seafarers. Many ships had orange trees as part of their standard load to keep the crew safe and healthy, or as healthy as you can be sailing across the ocean in the Late Middle Ages. The vitamin C produced by the orange, first the bitter one and then later the sweet orange that we know now, is important for a wide variety of health issues.

Until the introduction of vitamin C in tablet form, citrus fruits were the best way to receive a daily dose of the vitamin.

Orange wands are similar to other citrus and fruit wands. The are best for love and prosperity spells. Using an orange wand, cast a circle and stand in the middle. Take two oranges. Juice the oranges separately and take out the seeds. Place the seeds in two bowls, being careful not to mix them. Then, count the seeds from the first orange you juiced. That number will correspond with the letter in the alphabet that is the first letter of the first name of your intended. Do the same with the second orange. The letter that corresponds to that number is the first letter of the last name of your intended. Once you have counted and identified the initials of your soon-to-be love, close the circle and bury the seeds together by your front door. Your intended should arrive within a fortnight.

Osage Orange

ORDER: *Rosales*

FAMILY: *Moraceae*

GENUS: *Maclura*

SPECIES: *pomifera*

JANKA: 2040

ENERGY: Single life-giving force

ELEMENT(S): Earth

GOD(S) REPRESENTED: Wa-kon-tah

GODDESS(ES) REPRESENTED: Wa-kon-tah

When I lived in Oklahoma and Texas, osage orange trees were everywhere. They are used as windbreaks in fields and on golf courses. In the fall you had to play around the fruit that had fallen from the trees and been ripped apart by local squirrels for the seeds inside. The tree is often referred to as bois d'arc or horse apple, even though horses seldom eat their fruit. In fact, other than squirrels, no other animal eats the fruit on a regular basis. I've also been told that the fruit is poisonous to humans, although that has since been proven false. If you do consume an osage orange fruit, you will just *think* you are going to die—in actuality you'd probably just become violently sick and vomit the fruit back up.

The wood of the osage orange was used for fence posts throughout the central United States, and when I bought a Sears Craftsman kit house in Lawton, Oklahoma, the back fence posts were the original osage orange posts from the 1910s. They were pretty much rotted out, but what was left was so hard it was like working lignum or ironwood. Fresh osage orange is a good wood to work with, and to me at least it always feels moist no matter how long it dries. That may be why the posts lasted so long; they never dried out.

I enjoy the look of osage orange and use it when I can for walking sticks as well as wands. The wood darkens as it ages from a medium orange to a darker orange over time. While the wood is very useful, the fruit is not. The sap will cause mild skin irritation and will produce sickness in those who eat the fruit. There is a Lakota legend that says the osage orange's "brain fruit" is the result of a warrior who killed an old Lakota medicine man for his scalp. The old man was a favorite of the Creator Wakontanka, and once the warrior saw what he'd done and that the Creator was angry, he threw the medicine man's brain into the trees, where the Creator made it the fruit of the osage.

Wands of osage orange are good for guidance. Place a fruit of the osage orange on your altar, and with your wand cast your circle, calling on the Creator Wakontanka to bring you guidance and wisdom. Meditate on the fruit, and then cut it open and leave the seeds for the animals of the wood. Treat the rest of the fruit with honor and respect since it is the brain of the old medicine man.

Another use of the osage orange is as an insect repellant. Before the creation of insecticides, those living on the plains used the sap, although mildly irritating on the skin, as a pesticide. While this is not recommended today, you may cast your circle or perform your ritual with an orange osage wand and banish all pests from your presence. Remember to use the term "pest" for those who annoy/irritate you rather than the person's name.

Finally, osage orange bows are highly prized in the archery field. If you are a hunter, specifically a bow hunter, or an amateur archer on a team, the wand is very good for success spells before hunting or competition. If you hunt with a bow, make certain that you only invoke the spirits of the wand for food to each since all life is sacred.

Padauk (African)

ORDER: *Fabales*

FAMILY: *Fabaceae*

GENUS: *Pterocarpus*

SPECIES: *soyauxii*

JANKA: 1725

ENERGY: Female

ELEMENT(S): Fire

GOD(S) REPRESENTED: Nyambe

GODDESS(ES) REPRESENTED: Ala, Igbo

African padauk is a beautiful wood with bright yellow flowers that bloom in the middle of April, but there are many dark sides to this hardwood. The tree is found throughout Africa and Asia, and there are a number of species that are sold as padauk or mukwa (*Pterocarpus angolensis*), which is the native term for the wood. The wood is hard, porous, similar to palm in some ways with very small open pores, and very bright red. Although they are often mistaken in the wild as rosewoods, once they are felled or milled they may be easily discerned from the closer grained and more figurative rosewoods.

Initially, turning padauk is very easy, and the wood works well under a sharp chisel. However, if you are susceptible to skin irritation, specifically oils like urushiol, padauk is not a wood you want to work with. Many websites talk about the irritability of the wood for anyone who has easily aggravated skin. I am deathly allergic to poison ivy, which always worries my spouse when I work poison ivy wands. However, when I turned the padauk wand, I didn't realize the depth of the aggravation the dust would cause. One day I worked three wands, covering my hands with a fine red dust. I then cleaned up and played nine holes of golf. By that night I was covered in a poison ivy–type rash everywhere the dust had settled, and with open sores at my left wrist, which is where I take the brunt of the sanding dust from the lathe.

Uses for this wood vary. Some companies use it for decoration on xylophones and marimbas as well as neck inlays for guitars. Medically, the oil has been used to treat skin parasites and fungus infections, which is interesting considering what is does to some skin. But I guess what doesn't kill you makes you stronger.

Magically the problems I experienced are the reason you may want a padauk wand. While not life-threatening, the rashes caused by the padauk are highly annoying and distracting. The itch is unbelievable, and even after the rash subsides the itch remains. This wand, although not as strong as poison ivy, will cause distress to those against you when used for an annoyance or skin spell. Casting out from your circle, you may cause great temporary harm to those you wish to affect. If, however, you are being cast against, you may reverse the wand and use the base protect yourself from attack.

You may also use the wand positively with the head to assist others in healing rashes and the effects of other padauk or poison ivy wands by performing a counterspell. I have not heard of a successful spell of this type, though, due to the nature of first strike is first harm. It is always better to cast your defenses before someone else casts against you; but in that philosophy you are falling into wand escalation, similar to what some militaries use to justify more planes and soldiers. The call on this one is always yours.

Palm

ORDER: *Arecales*

FAMILY: *Arecaceae*

GENUS: *Sabal*

SPECIES: *spp*

JANKA: 1600

ENERGY: Masculine

ELEMENT(S): Air, Fire

GOD(S) REPRESENTED: Apollo

GODDESS(ES) REPRESENTED: Ashtoreth, Artemis, Isis, Diana, Ishtar

The palm tree is one that almost everyone recognizes worldwide. The coconuts, which are the fruit and the seed of the tree, may be found at any large grocery store, and the proliferation of palm trees throughout tropical or subtropical areas demonstrates the tree's determination to propagate. It's not hard to understand how widespread these trees are when you think that there are over 2,600 species scattered across the world.

Turning a palm wand is problematic at best. The trees have no real grain to them, but are rather fibrous. Therefore, trying to turn something such as a palm will end up pulling fibers from the stock. For that reason I recommend hand sanding with a delicate hand. Too much pressure and the wood will snap.

Magically the palm is good for survival in hot and tropical areas. The palm tree has evolved and survived for sixty million years in hostile environments and will give the user the same ability. While it is not recommended for northern magic, the palm will respond well to hot weather and tropical magic. To that end, the palm wand will move energies associated with oceans and dunes better than snowdrifts and ice.

Peach

ORDER: *Rosales*

FAMILY: *Rosaceae*

GENUS: *Prunus*

SPECIES: *persica*

JANKA: N/A

ENERGY: Feminine

ELEMENT(S): Earth

GOD(S) REPRESENTED: Momotaro
(demigod and cultural hero)

GODDESS(ES) REPRESENTED: Venus

The peach is a beautiful tree native to China and the Far East. The trees are moderate in height, and if they are like the tree that is in my front yard, they always bloom before the last frost. The wood is clear and has a lovely shape to it that makes the dwarf variety an especially good callout for specimen plantings in either front yards or backyards.

Peaches, similar to most other fruits, contain vitamin C, and as a member of the rose family, they have seeds that contain an amount of cyanogenic glycosides, which will upon decomposition create hydrogen cyanide gas. Thus, care should be taken around rotting peach pits.

The peach has historical significance all over Asia. The ancient Chinese believed that the peach granted vitality and vigor and helped to increase one's yang. The early leaders of China had their sorcerers wave a peach wand before them as they would process to protect them against evil spirits. In mythology the Chinese believed that peaches granted immortality. Their myth of the immortals eating peaches is told even today in the provinces. During the Feast of Peaches all the immortals would consume the fruit every six thousand years in a great hall. Also, in Chinese medicine peaches are used to reduce allergies and help blood flow.

One of Japan's greatest heroes, Momotarō ("Peach Boy"), was said to have been sent from heaven in a giant peach to be the child of a barren woman and her husband. When she opened the peach to eat it, the boy stepped out and explained he was there for them. Years later he went off to defeat evil spirits plaguing Japan, the *oni*, with a talking monkey, a pheasant, and a dog.

In Korea, the peach was given the ability to grant happiness, safety from evil, and longevity.

Peach wands are good for two very diverse actions. First, they are excellent for love spells and rituals (as are other fruit tree wands). Cast a circle and take a ripe peach and halve it. Extract the pit and plant it in a pot. Recite the following three times:

As this pit grows so shall my love.

Keep the pot warm and in the sun, give it ample amounts of food and water, and watch it grow. At the same time, be ever aware that your love is just around the corner and all it takes is some nurturing to bring your love to you.

The second use of a peach wand is exorcism. This is not to be confused with demonic possession, although I suppose you could do that also with a peach wand, but I'd want more backup. This exorcism is from ideas or baggage that you have cluttering up your life. Cast your circle and light a small fire in a brazier. On a piece of paper write what you are exorcising, or if you actually have some of the baggage in the form of papers or clothing, you may use that too. As the items burn in the brazier, concentrate on those things being out of your life forever. After the fire has burned out, bury the ashes at the farthest point from your front door. If you have access

THE WITCH'S GUIDE TO WANDS

to property farther away than your property, even better. As you cover over the ashes, say

I bury you never to return.

Your problems should be gone.

Pear (European)

ORDER: *Rosales*

FAMILY: *Rosaceae*

GENUS: *Pyrus*

SPECIES: *communis*

JANKA: N/A

ENERGY: Feminine

ELEMENT(S): Water

GOD(S) REPRESENTED: Cernunnos

GODDESS(ES) REPRESENTED: Venus

The pear is a native of Europe and Africa and has been prominent in the culture and foods of those areas for a few thousand years. Although thought to be of Chinese descent, the pear is now prevalent throughout the world, and you can find the major and hybridized versions at any farmers' market or grocery store. There are two types of pears, however, that are now grown: the fruiting pear and the Bradford pear. The fruiting pear, often referred to as the Bartlett pear, is a hybrid of the common European pear. The Bradford pear is a small fruiting species that bears fruit that is unuseable to humans but very beneficial to birds.

The pear turns as easily as other fruit trees, and the wood is very white. When turned, the different wands of fruit trees are very hard to discern from each other with the exception of the purple leaf plum, which has a distinctive wood pattern.

In Greek and Roman myth, pears are held sacred to the Goddesses Aphrodite, Hera, and Pomona. The pears are said to keep the Goddesses young and beautiful. Similarly, in Chinese mythology the pear, like the peach, is a symbol for immortality.

Magically, the pear is a symbol of love and lust, and pear wands are exceptional for those. Cunningham, in his *Encyclopedia of Magical Herbs*, says that witches once danced beneath pear trees, so if you have a pear wand, use it well and often.

Pecan

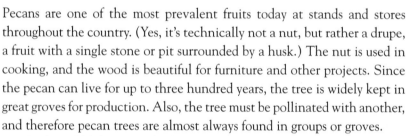

ORDER: *Fagales*

FAMILY: *Juglandaceae*

GENUS: *Carya*

SPECIES: *illinoinensis*

JANKA: 1780

ENERGY: Masculine

ELEMENT(S): Air

GOD(S) REPRESENTED: Mercury

GODDESS(ES) REPRESENTED: Priapus

Pecans are one of the most prevalent fruits today at stands and stores throughout the country. (Yes, it's technically not a nut, but rather a drupe, a fruit with a single stone or pit surrounded by a husk.) The nut is used in cooking, and the wood is beautiful for furniture and other projects. Since the pecan can live for up to three hundred years, the tree is widely kept in great groves for production. Also, the tree must be pollinated with another, and therefore pecan trees are almost always found in groups or groves.

Back in Oklahoma we had a number of pecan trees in our backyard and many more across the street in the empty lots. Every fall you could find my daughter and I picking the nuts along with other people. I have never liked pecans, but my mother would make pies with them, so every year she would get great bags of the shelled nuts that my dad husked for her. I think in the end he grew tired of both the pies and the work it took to get them ready for baking.

In Native American mythology the pecan is thought to be sacred to the Great Spirit. It is important to think of the commercial and religious value of the pecan when dealing with the power and energy of the wood in this kind of wand.

Pecan is a rather difficult wood to turn, but a pretty one. It takes a while to dry, though, and when trying to turn wet pecan the wood will gouge too easily to make it worth the work. Therefore, wait and be patient with the wood. You will appreciate that later.

Magically the pecan is good for money and employment. With your pecan wand cast a circle around yourself and whatever job advertisement you are interested in. Using a money draw or success oil, dress the four corners of the advertisement and roll it, tying it with a green ribbon. While concentrating on successfully gaining the job, burn the roll of paper in your brazier. Let the smoke wrap up around your wand. Then, once the fire is burned out, scatter the ashes at the four quarters of your circle while using the invoking pentagram. Continue to work toward your job and you should have positive results soon.

Persimmon (American)

ORDER: *Ericales*

FAMILY: *Ebenaceae*

GENUS: *Diospyros*

SPECIES: *virginiana*

JANKA: 2254

ENERGY: Feminine

ELEMENT(S): Water

GOD(S) REPRESENTED:
   Hermaphrodite

GODDESS(ES) REPRESENTED: Venus, Hermaphrodite

Persimmon is a member of the edible tree group. The fruit may be eaten cooked, dried, or raw, and is found throughout the world in one form or another. In the United States you will find the genus *virginiana* and the straight, rough-barked trees dot the southern and northern landscape in clumpings of many trees in one location, usually from fruit taking hold after dropping from the original tree.

The wood is clear and clean with a pleasant smell at cutting. It is slightly brittle, even though it is a hardwood, and will snap when cut down if you don't cut all the way through the tree. Even though the edible part is considered a fruit, it is actually a berry by botanical standards. If turned wet, the wood will cut in long spindles, and if you are trying to turn a piece of persimmon that is not perfectly straight, it is preferable to turn the wood freshly cut. Unfortunately, you will then have to finish the sanding later, after the wood dries, but if you don't cut off the endcaps, you should be able to remount the piece on the lathe and sand it appropriately.

Care should be taken if you eat the unripened fruit because the chemicals still in the fruit at that stage may react to other food in the stomach and produce lumps that can cause severe gastric distress. A home remedy uses Coca-Cola as an acid to dissolve these lumps, which in itself says something about Coke. The fruits should never be eaten on an empty stomach.

Commercially, the wood is used for pool cues and drumsticks as well as some handles for xylophone hammers. In golf the persimmon driver and fairway wood heads were one of the first to be manufactured in the United States and are collectable items now. The tree grows relatively quickly and are less prone to washout from heavy rains and floods than many other trees and shrubs. Therefore, it is used as a ground anchor in areas that have heavy rains or flooding.

Historically, the persimmon has been prominent for centuries. In the *Odyssey* the fruit in the land of the lotus eaters is thought to be the persimmon. The Native American tribes speak about the persimmon in a number of legends of distraction from the succulence of the fruit of the persimmon tree. Further, many tribes have used the bark and sap for medicinal purposes such as mouth ailments and throat injury. In fact, the name *persimmon* is probably a Powhatan word for "fruit of the tree."

Magically the persimmon is good for musical spells. Drummers who wish to excel in their craft may turn persimmon wands and then turn them into drumsticks. Further, if you cast a drum circle magically with a persimmon wand, you will have a deeper and more meaningful experience and be able to drum longer and better than without casting.

Persimmon is also excellent for water spells if you are concerned with areas that flood or may be damaged by high waters, such as low-level acreages. A spell cast with a persimmon wand and a fire using the cast-off chips and tendrils of the wood will assist you in averting a disaster; however, care must also be exercised in design and construction of swales, levees, and dams.

Persimmon is also the tree sacred to the Greek God(dess) Hermaphrodite. This wand, therefore, may be used by either gender effectively, and responds to Hermaphrodite in either his or her form. This wand is exceptionally well suited for transgender pagans, covens, rituals, or spells.

Pink Ivory

ORDER: *Rosales*

FAMILY: *Rhamnaceae*

GENUS: *Berchemia*

SPECIES: *zeyheri*

JANKA: 995

ENERGY: Masculine

ELEMENT(S): Fire

GOD(S) REPRESENTED: Gu

GODDESS(ES) REPRESENTED: Demeter, Nokhubulwane

Pink ivory is a very expensive and rare wood. The tree is native to southern Africa and was said to be sacred to the Zulu people, although that may have been a marketing ploy to increase the cost of the wood once it was made publicly available. I find it interesting that even though most sites list the wood as rare and the cost of a small piece is quite high, the natives of Mozambique us the wood for fence poles. That always seemed out of place to me in the world market.

The fruit of the tree is similar to a plum and is eaten either fresh from the tree or dried, similar to prunes and dried apricots, supplying nutrition in leaner months. The bark of the mature tree is used to make purple dye.

Magically the tree is very good for healing. The bark may be powdered to cure headaches and back pain. When using a pink ivory wand for healing, cast your circle with the individual in pain sitting comfortably in a chair in the center of the circle. Next, place the wand in the individual's hands, head pointed down between the legs, with no obstruction to the ground. As you perform your circle to relieve the pain, direct all the pain through the individual and then through the wand to be dispersed into the ground, where it will do no harm. Once the ritual is finished, have the individual hold the wand firmly in his or her left hand and snap it toward the ground to clear all residual sickness or illness from the wand. Then you may use the wand to close the circle.

Plum (Cherry)

ORDER: *Rosales*

FAMILY: *Rosaceae*

GENUS: *Prunus*

SPECIES: *cerasifera*

JANKA: 1550

ENERGY: Feminine

ELEMENT: Water

GODS: Liber, Picumnus

GODDESSES: Venus

The cherry plum, also called the purple leaf plum, is a common tree in many parks, golf courses, and home yards. The deep purple of the leaves gives a good specimen to the yard, and with a corresponding Japanese maple will set off a deep green lawn or flowerbed. My next-door neighbor has a purple-leaf that has been allowed to grow straight up instead of being trimmed into its traditional lollipop shape, which has detracted from its look.

I enjoy the cherry plum because of its fruit. The plums are very small and very sour. They seldom get larger than a quarter or a Kennedy half dollar (I'm showing my age, right?), and with the pit there is little flesh and skin to eat, but they are very tasty and if you collect enough of them they make a delicious jam or jelly.

The wand I turned in cherry plum was green. As soon as I stopped turning the wood, it would take on a dark orange hue. That was from the sap, and eventually it mellowed out as I sanded it, but the appearance was quite striking. The wood turns similar to all other fruit trees. It is a clean wood to turn, and when wet, produces long tendrils.

Cherry plum wands are good for jelly makers and candymakers. They are similar to the persimmon wands in that the energy from the wood that produces so many fruits will carry over to the magic of the food. I would also turn kitchen spoons from cherry plum to add to the magical aspect of the jelly. There are so many of these trees around my area that finding a piece large enough to carve into a small wooden spoon is not difficult. To make a spoon wand, cut down your wand blank to a point and then leave a larger section for the spoon. One the handle is turned you may carve out the spoon section by hand or with hand tools. Finally, turn the end of the handle as the head of your wand, and you have a spoon wand for cooking and casting in the kitchen. While this works well with any fruit wood, I would say that plum, cherry, apple, or peach might work best.

Poplar

See Aspen.

Purpleheart

ORDER: *Fabales*

FAMILY: *Fabaceae*

GENUS: *Peltogyne*

SPECIES: *spp*

JANKA: 1860

ENERGY: Feminine

ELEMENTS: Air

GOD(S): Agwu, Eshmun, Haoma

GODDESS(ES): Ala

Purpleheart is a medium hardwood that looks brown until it is cut and polished and then takes on a deep purple color with tight grain. The wood turns well with sharp tools and sands up with minimum scratching. There are two types of purpleheart that I have found in wood suppliers—oftentimes in the same bin. One is a finer grain and is the best for wands. The other is a coarser-grained wood and does not sand or turn as well. So when you look at purpleheart, make certain the grain is tight and there are no splinters or jagged edges. Some species of purpleheart are becoming overharvested, so be careful where and how much you purchase. The wood is also called amaranth and oftentimes listed as that in books such as Cunningham's *Encyclopedia of Magical Herbs*.

The Purple Heart is a badge of military merit. Originally designed in 1780 as a medal for unusual gallantry, it was later changed to signify wounds sustained in combat. The Purple Heart originally had "Merit" written on it and was awarded to foster and encourage every act of military merit.

Because of this, the purpleheart wand is exceptionally well-suited for courage and self-sacrifice. Spells cast with the purpleheart wand will exhibit extraordinary power to change and encourage the individual to do great deeds and make dire sacrifices if necessary. The wand is also adept at healing unseen wounds, such as psychological ones derived through combat or other traumatic situations.

Purpleheart is good at protection, and spells cast with a purpleheart wand will protect the user throughout the year. Legend has it that a full amaranth plant wrapped in a white cloth will protect its user against bullets, although I suspect it's prudent to treat these as metaphoric bullets and not literal ones. Use the wand to cast a circle around you as you move through your year to protect yourself against those who would do you harm. Carry amaranth flowers in a small cachet to add protection.

Redheart

ORDER: *Gentianales*

FAMILY: *Rubiaceae*

GENUS: *Simira*

SPECIES: *sickingia salvadorensis*

JANKA: 1200

ENERGY: Feminine

ELEMENT(S): Fire

GOD(S): Bolon Dxacab

GODDESS(ES): Ixchel

The redheart (also called chakte kok) is a medium to tall tree with a pitch that turns bright red upon contact with the air. In this regard the wood is then turned red when cut and milled. Unfortunately, the wood will fade to a yellowish brown if left in the sun too long, so protection of the wood is always advisable. This is another example of a wood being referred to as something else. Throughout the Central American states the wood is commonly referred to as either Cuban or Dominican mahogany, thus confusing many dealers as to what they are actually purchasing and receiving.

The wood turns very well and produces dark and bright red chips when being worked. However, be careful when sanding, because the dust is dark and invasive and will stick to everything, and you may find yourself coated in it. It is also very heavy, so be extra careful to wear protective masks over your mouth and nose as well as eye protection.

Magically this wand will perform a variety of duties. It is good for blood work since, like blood, the sap and wood turn red upon contact with the air, although a bloodwood/satine wand is the primary wand used for blood rituals. Wands of redheart excel, though, at cardio work, either to help heal or to help prevent heart ailments. Used in conjunction with your doctor's recommendations, this wand will help you get through the most difficult situations as effectively as possible.

If you do turn the wand, keep the shavings separated to be used in your brazier during ritual. Burning the shavings will assist in the ritual and add force to whatever you are requesting.

Rosewood (East Indian)

ORDER: *Fabales*

FAMILY: *Fabaceae*

GENUS: *Dalbergia*

SPECIES: *latifolia*

JANKA: 2200

ENERGY: Feminine

ELEMENT(S): Air

GOD(S): Varuna

GODDESS(ES): Saranyu

East Indian rosewood is one of a number of rosewoods found throughout the tropical Americas, Madagascar, and around Southeast Asia. The East Indian variety is a deep purple and considered one of the classical versions. While some rosewoods have been overforested and are on the endangered species list, the East Indian variety is still available from reputable dealers. It is also important to note that not all rosewoods are actually rosewoods. Many dealers of exotic woods will add a place or locale to a wood and call it a rosewood when in actuality it may be a different species. Therefore, care is paramount.

East Indian rosewood is a very hard and dense wood that turns well with sharp tools. It sands to a high polish and shines when a light coat of polish or oil is applied. The deep, dark purples are reminiscent of purpleheart, but there is a more splotchy makeup to the pattern. It is import-ant to note that not all *Dalbergia* are rosewoods; some, such as cocobolo

(*Dalbergia retusa*) and Brazilian tulipwood (*Dalbergia decipularis*) are in the same genus but are not considered part of the rosewood species.

Magically East Indian rosewood is ideal for board game magic—specifically chess. The dark pieces that are almost black in nature are often used in chess pieces and a spell or ritual for success in board games will be more powerful with a wand of this wood. This is also another good wood for musicians, specifically string musicians such as guitar players. The Gibson guitar company has used rosewood for some of their higher-end guitars for many decades. Further, this wood will work well for those suffering breathing problems if the base is used. Since the dust of the rosewoods are irritants to breathing, the base of the wand may assist the individual in protecting his or her lungs, although this is no substitute for medical attention, which should be sought if breathing issues continue. I have emphysema and must use a mask whenever I turn or sand any type of wood, but especially when I work on rosewoods.

Rosewood (Yucatan)

ORDER: *Fabales*

FAMILY: *Fabaceae*

GENUS: *Dalbergia*

SPECIES: *yucatensis*

JANKA: 1560

ENERGY: Feminine

ELEMENT(S): Air

GOD(S): Bolon Dzacab

GODDESS(ES): Bastet, Pasht, Ubasti

Yucatan rosewood is a less dense, although just slightly so, cousin of the East Indian variety. The dust that is produced during sanding of this wood is also less aggravating, and if you want a nice variated pattern of yellows, oranges, and browns, then this wood is a good choice. The Yucatan rosewood is also used for guitars and therefore acceptable for musicians and those who play guitars specifically.

There are some experts in the field who question whether this is actually a rosewood. The end grain is not representative of most other rosewoods, and the oils that are produced by the wood are lower than other rosewoods, thus making it a better wood to turn and sand. If you are looking for color, this is a good choice. If you are looking for a specific musical choice for magic, then this is also an acceptable choice over the East Indian rosewood. However, depending on your needs, you should spend some time with each variety to determine which speaks to you most.

Rowan (American Mountain Ash)

ORDER: *Rosales*

FAMILY: *Rosaceae*

GENUS: *Sorbus*

SPECIES: *americana*

JANKA: 1010

ENERGY: Feminine

ELEMENT(S): Earth, Fire

CELTIC OGHAM: Luis

GOD(S) REPRESENTED: Thor, Vulcan

GODDESS(ES) REPRESENTED:
    Aphrodite, Brigid, Cerridwen, Hebe, Hecate

The rowan is also called the American mountain ash or serviceberry, even though the serviceberry is an entirely different tree, and that is most likely how you will find it listed if you are lucky enough to find a store that has it. The confusion develops from the traditional names of the species as wild service tree or true service tree, and these have translated to the general public as serviceberry. It has been the most elusive wood to procure in this entire list of woods. The true rowan is found in the upper regions of the

United States and in Canada. Rowan is a weaker version of the ash and is therefore not used much for building or arts and crafts work. The easiest way to identify the tree is by its berries that form in large, bright red clusters in the fall and remain that way throughout the winter.

In mythology the rowan has a long history. The Goddess Hebe used rowan to create rejuvenating liquids for the Gods to keep them young and fertile. In Norse myth the first woman was created from a rowan tree, and the rowan saved Thor's life when he was being swept into Niflheim. The druids were said to use the bark as a black dye for their magical robes.

Magically the rowan is a powerful wood. A wand made of rowan will give its user the ability to call to the Gods of many different traditions and paths. The rowan wand is excellent for use against enchantment and those using witchcraft against you. It is a great wand for writers or orators when they need to express themselves in a better way. The wand is used also for fertility and healing of both old and new wounds.

When using the rowan for expression, practice your oratory or poetry while holding the wand and directing the words out through the wood. As you work through your prose or verse, think of how the wand moves with the words, forming patterns and rhythms. Once you are satisfied with the final product, practice again without the wand in your hand but remembering how the wand worked back and forth. This will give you more power to control your audience and hold them under your sway.

Sapele

ORDER: *Sapindales*

FAMILY: *Meliaceae*

GENUS: *Entandrophragma*

SPECIES: *cylindricum*

JANKA: 1510

ENERGY: Masculine

ELEMENT(S): Air

GOD(S) REPRESENTED: Selvans

GODDESS(ES) REPRESENTED: Nei Tituaabine, Kiribati

Sapele is an African hardwood similar to some species of mahogany. The wood is harvested for musical instruments and car interiors. It is also used where grain is important for fine furniture and fixtures. The wood is protected in many sections of Africa, and farms are starting to be organized to keep the wood in production without endangering the local wild stands.

Working with this wood is easy. The hardness of the wood and the tightness of the grain lend themselves well to turning and sanding, and the wood takes a light olive oil or Scott's Liquid Gold seal, which brings out the nuances of the piece.

Magically the sapele is used for healing and divination. Wands of this wood will successfully cast circles for visioning and rituals that involve looking through the Aether in Steampunk Magic, as well as beyond the veil, in traditional magical paths. If you are a classic car collector or classic car race enthusiast, a sapele wand will assist you in winning your heat or your classification. Also, this wood is good for musical spells that revolve around stringed instruments, specifically the guitar, ukulele, and pitch box.

Sumac

ORDER: *Sapindales*

FAMILY: *Anacardiaceae*

GENUS: *Rhus*

SPECIES: *coriaria*

JANKA: 680

ENERGY: Masculine

ELEMENT(S): Fire

GOD(S) REPRESENTED: Huehueteotl

GODDESS(ES) REPRESENTED: Cihuacoatl, Chantico

Sumac (commonly called elm-leaved sumac, tanner's sumac, or Sicilian sumac) should not be confused with poison sumac, which is in the *Toxicodendron* genus along with poison oak and poison ivy. This sumac is a benign shrub that will at times grow to be eight to ten feet tall. The sumac is identified by its bright red fruit in the fall, which is used in cooking and making flavored drinks. Most sumacs are found growing wild along the sides of roads or where forests have been opened to form planted fields or sports fields.

The fruit is used in spices when dried and ground and is popular in many dishes prepared throughout the Middle East. In the United States the berries are used to brew a tea or ade similar to lemonade. Cold brewing and straining will ultimately result in a drink that may be sweetened with sugar or another sweetener and consumed during the warm months.

Magically sumac will connect to the earth and the fire of the planet. A wand of sumac is difficult to make because the wood is so soft it almost crumbles when dried. Extreme care must be taken when sanding a sumac wand. The wand, though, will be very useful in harnessing fields and the borders of open ranges, and if used in a protection spell, it will keep the creatures of the forest from your fields and the produce of your fields from wandering into the forest.

Sweetgum

ORDER: *Saxifragales*

FAMILY: *Altingiaceae*

GENUS: *Liquidambar*

SPECIES: *styraciflua*

JANKA: 850

ENERGY: Masculine

ELEMENT(S): Fire

GOD(S) REPRESENTED: Winalagalis

GODDESS(ES) REPRESENTED: Nuxalk, Qamaits

Sweetgum is a nuisance tree in most areas. The "gumball" that is the seed-pod becomes a missile when caught in snow or lawn mowers. For that reason many cities have banned them from common areas such as parks and roadways. The trees also throw up knees that become a hazard to pedestrians and lawn care equipment. However, the dangers of the plant notwithstanding, the wood itself is a lovely light yellow that works well and looks attractive in furniture and other projects. The tree is easily identified by its five-pointed leaf and the aforementioned pods.

The tree is a breeding ground for certain caterpillars and therefore has a positive reason for plantings if they are placed outside common walking or driving areas. Medically the tree has been used since the sixth century by the Chinese for blood and chi work, and the sap of the American version is said to be good for sciatica by kitchen witches in the South. Finally, the hardened sap is used as a chewing gum in many southern states to this day.

Magically the wand of a sweetgum tree may be used for increased spiritual or magical energy, drawing the chi from the Aether from within the user or around him or her. The wand may also be used in healing rituals where blood or nerves are concerned. Cast a circle with sweetgum and call upon the earth quarter to ground the nerves and steady them for the future. You may also cast a circle and call upon the south quarter to stimulate the blood and heat it up to grant more energy and longevity.

For defense the wand may be used base end outward to ward off projectiles thrown from others—either physical projectiles such as hail or sleet or metaphysical projectiles such as negative energies or spells. If you hold the base of the wand and use the head to cast, you may throw projectiles at your enemies in the same way. However, as in any other casting, whatever you send out will return to you threefold, so be aware before casting anything toward anyone.

Sycamore

ORDER: *Proteales*

FAMILY: *Platanaceae*

GENUS: *Platanus*

SPECIES: *occidentalis*

JANKA: 770

ENERGY: Feminine

ELEMENT(S): Air, Water

GOD(S) REPRESENTED: Osiris

GODDESS(ES) REPRESENTED:
Hathor, Isis, Nut

The sycamore is one of the more distinctive trees due to its bark, which peels and flakes off the trunk in large pieces, reminiscent of a peeling sunburn. The sycamore is a very large tree oftentimes growing as high as 130 feet and almost 6 feet in diameter. The wood is used for butcher blocks and crating. Also, in a pinch the wood will be used for furniture and house siding.

Working with sycamore is very easy. The wood is soft and turns well, sanding very similar to pine and other coniferous species, even though it is deciduous. I treat the sycamore the same as basswood and poplar. Expect a soft wood and be a little more careful with bounce, although most of the time I don't experience it.

A Cherokee legend says that the Gods gave the animals of the world fire in the hollowness of a sycamore tree. Many animals attempted to bring back the fire from the inside of the tree because it was sealed and surrounded by water. Eventually the water spider spun a web and harnessed one small piece of the burning tree and brought it back in a bowl on its back. The animals of the world had fire, and the spider to this day has a bright red bowl shape on its back.

Magically the sycamore is good for divination and prosperity. A wand of sycamore will cut through the Aether to show what is actually out there instead of the nuances and false trails that are oftentimes found while working in the Aether. For this particular ritual you'll be using your wand as a dowser. Cast your circle at sunset without lights. As the sun sets and it gets almost too dark to see, place the wand in your open left palm. Thinking of what you are trying to divine, turn slowly in a clockwise manner. When the wand tells you to stop (and it may take more than one revolution to reach that point), look past the head of the wand and out into the now dark Aether. Your answers and realizations should be out there for you to see and take note of.

Tamarind

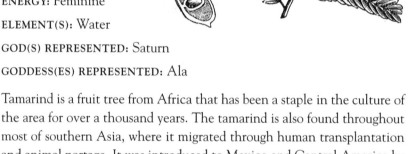

ORDER: *Fabales*

FAMILY: *Fabaceae*

GENUS: *Tamarindus*

SPECIES: *indica*

JANKA: 2318

ENERGY: Feminine

ELEMENT(S): Water

GOD(S) REPRESENTED: Saturn

GODDESS(ES) REPRESENTED: Ala

Tamarind is a fruit tree from Africa that has been a staple in the culture of the area for over a thousand years. The tamarind is also found throughout most of southern Asia, where it migrated through human transplantation and animal portage. It was introduced to Mexico and Central America by the Spanish invaders and has remained an important economical product ever since.

The culinary uses of the tamarind fruit are almost endless. It is used throughout the world in salads, candies, meat sauces, carbonated beverages, soups, jams, and sauces. The fruit and pulp may be also used as a topical antiseptic, since the same chemical components are also active in brass and copper polishes. Finally, if you ingest too much tamarind, the effect is that of a commercial laxative.

Tamarind is a hardwood that feels almost brittle and chips easily under chisels. The wood does not form long tendrils when on a lathe, but rather very small chips that come off the blank in large quantities. However, the wood does not bounce much unless you hit a knot or other scar in the wood, allowing the turner to work the wood quickly, and it sands very well with little effort.

Mythologically, the tamarind is credited with having very small leaves because of a battle between the Hindu God Bhasmasura, who was in charge of the Demon Army called the Asura and Shiva. In his arrogance he challenged Shiva to a fight to the death. Shiva accepted the challenge and wounded Bhasmasura so severely that the demon ran away and hid himself in the leaves and branches of the tamarind tree, which at that time were large and plentiful. Failing to find his foe, Shiva opened his third eye and saw Bhasmasura in the tree. With a blast of energy he destroyed the demon, but in the process he shattered all the leaves, forever changing their growth pattern to small and seemingly broken.

Magically the fruit of the tamarind is used in poultices and potions. A wand of tamarind will give its wielder power to influence feasts and picnics as well as cause others the loss of such abilities. A ritual cast at a full moon with a tamarind wand will cause the cooks to prosper in their endeavors.

Teak

ORDER: *Lamiales*

FAMILY: *Lamiaceae*

GENUS: *Tectona*

SPECIES: *grandis*

JANKA: 1155

ENERGY: Feminine

ELEMENT(S): Water

GOD(S) REPRESENTED: Wuluwaid

GODDESS(ES) REPRESENTED: Djunkgao

Teak is a popular tree for furniture and other creations that require a hardwood with a fine finish. The tree originates in the Pacific Rim of Indonesia but has since been cultivated across the world in tropical climates. In Central America many other trees are being called teak since they look similar and it's easier to call something that is unidentified teak and sell it than have a tree left. This misnaming of teak, as was noted with rosewood, accounts for much of the false labeling across the industry.

Teak is hard but turns well on a lathe. The natural oils keep the wood slightly damp, although it is oftentimes difficult to feel the dampness unless you are used to it. When I sand the wood, it feels similar to soap on my fingertips. It's just a feeling, but it's significant enough that you don't forget the feeling after experiencing it. The wood is good for construction that requires outdoor use or where there are damaging insects such as termites or ants. The natural oils keep the wood from being attacked, and it is therefore used in many places as pillars and pilings for bridges and houses. Teak has also been used for hundreds of years in the boatbuilding industry since it is a durable wood in water. Many of today's finer motorboats are made of teak.

Magically teak is very good for boating or travel safety by water. A teak wand will cast a powerful spell in circle to keep you safe and secure while traveling over water. The wand is also useful if you are planning an outside event such as a picnic or house party. Cast a permeable circle around your house and yard, or wherever you are having your get-together, and call upon your specific Gods or Goddesses to protect those at the party from harm and problems. Remember to take down the circle after everyone has left.

THE WITCH'S GUIDE TO WANDS

Tulip Tree

ORDER: *Magnoliales*

FAMILY: *Magnoliaceae*

GENUS: *Liriodendron*

SPECIES: *tulipifara*

JANKA: 950

ENERGY: Feminine

ELEMENT(S): Water

GOD(S) REPRESENTED: Chiron, Paeon

GODDESS(ES) REPRESENTED: Artemis, Hygieia

The tulip tree is the fastest-growing hardwood in the East that maintains its structural strength and integrity as it grows, unlike the cottonwood and other fast-growing species. The wood is a clear wood that has tight grain, giving it its strength for woodworking and floorings. The leaves of the tulip tree are easy to recognize by their size and heart shape.

The tulip tree is exceptional as a specimen tree for landscape architects and designers for its quick growth rate and distinctive leaf pattern. The flowers are tulip-shaped and form a thick covering to the tree, giving the owners a breathtaking sight if planted correctly. Care for the tree is simple; well-draining and thick topsoil and low salt are best for these; therefore, they don't do well in low, marshy areas on the coasts. The more sun the tree receives the lower it will grow to the ground, making it an excellent choice as a small display piece. However, if the tree is planted in a shaded area the growth will go vertical instead of horizontal, and the full measure of trunk will display in up to forty feet of new tree in just under twenty years.

The tulip tree is known by many other names, the most popular one being poplar. While many other trees are also referred to as poplar (see the Aspen entry, e.g.), this is another example of a name being applied that isn't really accurate but popular. Because of the misnomer it is sold as a furniture material and buyers think they are purchasing a true poplar instead of the real wood, even though both are equally strong and attractive when stained.

Magically the tree is good for healing when the wand is used in conjunction with the bark made into a tea. It is also good for brewing spells and rituals, since the roots of the tulip tree are used in some breweries to flavor the beer. Cast a circle with a tulip tree wand during your initial preparation process and you will have a good yield of beer or ale.

Walnut (Black)

ORDER: *Fagales*

FAMILY: *Juglandaceae*

GENUS: *Juglans*

SPECIES: *nigra*

JANKA: 1010

ENERGY: Masculine

ELEMENT(S): Air, Fire

GOD(S) REPRESENTED: Thor, Vishnu, Zeus

GODDESS(ES) REPRESENTED: Artemis, Aphrodite, Astarte, Diana, Hel

Black walnut is a curious wood. It is very durable and tough. I made a black walnut coffee table thirty years ago, and it's still as pristine as the day it came out of the Army woodshop in Texas. It's just that difficult to dent, break, or damage. However, it is also a dangerous wood as I mentioned in the introduction. The chemical juglone is released from the tree's leaves, fruit, and bark. When the juglone falls, it sets up a ring around the tree that is fatal to some plants, such as tomatoes and peppers. Also, when the pollen begins to settle on the skin, it can aggravate the pores and cause contact dermatitis as well as breathing problems if it is inhaled.

So why then would anyone want a wand from black walnut? Because the reasons you may not want one in your yard are the exact reasons you may want one on your altar. Its durability coupled with its power to harm or cause sickness is a perfect combination for someone defending against an external spell or ritual.

While I do not advocate harming others as a first strike, I do support throwing back what is sent your way. With a black walnut wand you can perform protection spells, unlike most other wands, because of the specific properties of the juglones. Finally, if you are trying to avoid pregnancy, the use of the black walnut wand may put off your getting pregnant, although there may be other better ways available. Remember, nothing is perfect or guaranteed.

When using the black walnut wand as a positive instrument, you will use the head for protection against sickness or pregnancy. If, though, you are trying to defend against someone casting a spell against you, then you would reverse the wand: holding the head, use the base as you cast your spell or perform your ritual.

Wenge

ORDER: *Fabales*

FAMILY: *Fabaceae*

GENUS: *Millettieae*

SPECIES: *laurentii*

JANKA: 1630

ENERGY: Masculine

ELEMENT(S): Earth

GOD(S) REPRESENTED: Pluto

GODDESS(ES) REPRESENTED: Hel

Wenge is a dark, almost black, wood that grows in tropical climates. The wood has a very fine and hairy grain that is similar to palm. Because the wood is so dense, it is a perfect source for flooring and other construction pieces where an overcoat is applied. Care is advised when handling this wood due to splinters festering quickly and becoming infected.

I don't like working with wenge. Although it's a lovely wood to turn and the grains are exquisite, the wood itself is horrid unless you plan on sealing it with a varnish or polyurethane. The wood is similar to black palm and is fibrous. Therefore, no matter how much you sand it there will be splinters against the grain to catch your material and skin. The first wenge wand I turned I used Scott's Liquid Gold, and it didn't help much. For the next wand, as an experiment, I used clear sealing wax. I put it on at high speed and with the back of a sanding belt melted and sealed the wax into the wand. Note: I left the base and tip unwaxed so as not to disrupt the energy flow. Even that didn't completely solve the splinter problem, however.

Wenge is another musically inclined wood. Guitar makers as well as other stringed instrument makers use wenge for their frets and bodies. It is also very popular for bowls and other large items on the lathe when mixed with a lighter-colored wood, such as maple or birch.

Magically wenge is similar to poison ivy. The dust thrown off when sanding will cause contact dermatitis; not as serious as the radicans, but significant enough to be cautious of it. A wand of wenge will cast skin conditions to others and may be used to disrupt team sports or singular opponents through rashes and itching. The dust, once in contact with the eyes, will cause severe irritation, and spells cast with a wenge wand will cause others to lose sight of you or their goals, thus giving you the upper hand in business or sports.

White Willow

ORDER: *Malpighiales*

FAMILY: *Salicaceae*

GENUS: *Salix*

SPECIES: *alba*

JANKA: 580

ENERGY: Feminine

ELEMENT(S): Fire,
    Water

CELTIC OGHAM: Sail

GOD(S) REPRESENTED: Loki, Poseidon, Zeus

GODDESS(ES) REPRESENTED: Artemis, Athena, Brigid, Cerridwen, Hel,
    The Morrigan, Ishtar

White willow is a great tree to have a wand of. It is often referred to as a weeping willow because of the way the boughs and limbs droop from the weight of the branches. You may find the white willow as well as other species of the genus *Salix* near water since it is a very thirsty tree and will grow geometrically by the amount of water it gets. Planting willows in wet ground will ensure you have very large trees, but that isn't always a positive trait. The willow, similar to other fast-growing trees, is also a very short-lived tree, and once the tree begins to die, the limbs become problematic to anyone or anything under them.

The tree is also very messy. In the fall the fine leaves form a thick carpet inches thick on the ground. If close to water, these falls may clog drains and waterways to the point of flooding if something as small as a leafy branch begins stopping the flow. I bought a piece of property once in Oklahoma that had a severe drainage issue in the backyard. The previous owner planted a bald cypress and a white willow within eight feet of each other, and in the few years he owned the house the cypress grew to be over forty feet tall and the willow over twenty feet. In the fall there was nothing that could be grown or even mowed in that section of the yard for all the detritus on the ground.

Medicinally the white willow was one of the first headache powders. The ground bark of the willow contains salicin, which is what salicylic acid is derived from. Salicylic acid is the principal ingredient of aspirin and other such medicines. You may find white willow powder in many homeopathy stores and natural drugstores around the world. In Greco-Roman history many scholars, from Hippocrates and Galen to Pliny the Elder, touted the effectiveness of white willow bark, and the powder could be found being traded and sold throughout the Middle East at times as far back as the height of the Egyptian, Sumerian, and Assyrian cultures.

Magically the healing properties of willow are utmost. Headaches and general malaise are the two most important areas of the wand turned from willow. If possible, find a smaller but stout wand piece, and leave the bark on the base of the wand. That way you have the benefit of the willow bark when casting healing spells. If that is not possible, then think about imbedding a piece of the bark into the base of the wand.

Another use of the wand is for cricket. Willow has been hybridized as a cricket bat wood because it is straight, strong, and doesn't splinter. I would not recommend the wand be used for any other sporting event, though, since cricket is a rather specific sport and does not translate well to other field sports, even those similar to it.

Yellowheart

ORDER: *Sapindales*

FAMILY: *Rutaceae*

GENUS: *Euxylophora*

SPECIES: *paraensis*

JANKA: 1790

ENERGY: Masculine

ELEMENT(S): Earth, Air, Fire, Water

GOD(S) REPRESENTED: Chaos

GODDESS(ES) REPRESENTED: Eris

Yellowheart is a large tree found in and around Brazil. It is a tall tree, sometimes over 120 feet, with strong roots and a clear yellow heartwood.

The wood is easy to work and turns well with moderately sharpened tools. The grain is so tight that it almost feels plastic at times, giving a wand of yellowheart an ethereal quality.

Being a chaotic wood, yellowheart is good for chaos magic according to many who use it. Meditation, healing, and creativity spells work well with this wood since even though it is "scattered" and chaotic in nature it is a positive wood, and it will give you good results if it is properly used in castings.

For success spells use this wand as a disruptor to others' organizational abilities—individuals or teams. For example, request in your ritual that an opposing team loses hope or interest and quits. You may also request that the players leave the field or, better yet, never show up to the game. The failure of an opposing team or individual is important to this wood since it is associated with fear and failure.

Zebrawood

ORDER: *Fabales*

FAMILY: *Fabaceae*

GENUS: *Microberlinia*

SPECIES: *brazzavillensis*

JANKA: 1575

ENERGY: Feminine

ELEMENT(S): Air

GOD(S) REPRESENTED: Iroas, Zoran

GODDESS(ES) REPRESENTED: Danu, Debranua

Zebrawood is a beautiful wood to work with, having dark stripes against a light background. For this reason the term *zebrawood* was first used in the late 1700s and the wood became a popular species for furniture makers and cabinetmakers. The wood has since developed into a very good wood for flooring and other hardwood uses, such as trim and molding. Grown in the same region as Central American rosewoods, this tree's name has had a number of permutations. The original trees from Honduras and Nicaragua were augmented by a similar genus and species from Brazil, and these two are now interchangeable at times at wood and hobby shops.

Zebrawood is ideal to work with on a lathe if you have sharp tools. It turns well, takes a good sand, and shines up nicely under oils. The sharp contrast of the stripes to background give the wands made from this wood an attractive appearance, and the wood is able to be shaped into intricate designs.

Magically the wood is said to be good for creativity and love. It is also a good wand to use for wisdom and during divinations. However, its best use is for sports and escape. The wand is useful for large sporting events, when fleetness and speed are essential, such as soccer, football, and la-crosse. The wand is also recommended for flight—not as in air flight, but rather flight from danger. The wood was named originally for its similari-ties to an actual zebra, and the wood emulates that ability of speed, agility, and escape excellently.

Use of this wand is recommended in rituals for success in competitions of speed and agility. The wand will react well to these requirements and should give you the edge required to excel at such endeavors. However, as with all spells and rituals, the wand cannot overcome all obstacles without help. Proper training and knowledge must also be applied, and that will eventually give you the wisdom to overcome your opponents or enemies.

Zelkova

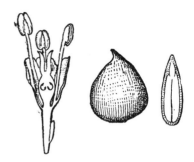

ORDER: *Rosales*

FAMILY: *Ulmaceae*

GENUS: *Zelkova*

SPECIES: *serrata*

JANKA: 1040

ENERGY: Masculine

ELEMENT(S): Earth

GOD(S) REPRESENTED: Selvans

GODDESS(ES) REPRESENTED: Zeme

The zelkova is an elm tree native to southern Europe and East Asia. They may be as small as shrubs or extremely large trees depending on their plantings and purpose. The zelkova on the Clemson campus are full grown and ring the inner courtyard of one of the academic buildings. The tree is useful specifically as a specimen tree due to the possibly attractive bark when mature. The splotchiness of the external bark augmented by the darker brown of the inner bark gives the tree an interesting texture.

Because of its nature and growth rate, the hardwood zelkova is used often in furniture where support and strength matters. The name zelkova is taken from the Georgian name Dzelkva, meaning "rock" and "bar," where the wood is used in the building trade. Turning the wood, even wet, is a chore, and once the wood dries and hardens, the chisels must be extremely sharp or the wood will skim. Once you get the shape of the wand cut, though, the sanding process is about the same as any other wood of its hardness and the finish is quite lovely.

Magically the zelkova is a limited wood. Carpenters may use a wand made from zelkova to strengthen their constructions and cast a strength circle, but that is about all there is to this very pretty and very hard wood. However, the most important use of zelkova is for taiko drums. The Japanese have used the ancient zelkova trees for their immense drums for hundreds of years.

Deciduous Shrubs, Vines, Grasses, and Roots

Deciduous shrubs are those that lose their leaves in the fall but are not large enough to be considered a true tree. Fig and crepe myrtle are excellent examples of this grouping. The fig, although very large when mature, and having solid branching, is still not a tree since it has multiple stalks that fill out rather than rise above. Crepe myrtle is another prime example. The crepe myrtle in the Midwest is a very small and scrubby shrub seldom growing over four to six feet in height and acts more as a shrub or hedge. However, in the Southeast the crepe myrtle may reach tree proportion with large multiple trunks from a central core and reaching heights in excess of twenty feet. It really is in the presentation at times.

Vines, on the other hand, may also be used as wands, although they are usually crafted by hand. Examples are grape, wisteria, and poison ivy. The leaves fall in the colder months, making them deciduous, and they work very well as wands if properly prepared and maintained. The Celts assigned the letter M or *Muin* to the vine, and I would imagine it was the grapevine they were referring to. Similar to that, the Celts assigned the letter G or *Gort* to ivy, and even though it was most likely the ground ivies that they were discussing, it could have been the more poisonous ones, too.

The only grass in this grouping is bamboo. While there is new evidence that bamboo is no longer a grass, there is also enough evidence to show that the growth pattern and other characteristics of this invasive plant may remain in the grass category. I am not a horticulturalist, so I will not be the final word on this.

Finally, there are roots. Licorice root is a prime example. The root is the product of the plant, and the root is what conducts the energy and the magic. Turning a wand from a root is no different than turning a wand from any other piece of the plant. It just takes time and attention to magical detail.

Bamboo (Golden)

ORDER: *Poales*

FAMILY: *Poaceae*

GENUS: *Bambusa*

SPECIES: *vulgaris*

JANKA: 1400

ENERGY: Masculine

ELEMENT(S): Air

GOD(S) REPRESENTED: Thoth

GODDESS(ES) REPRESENTED: Izanami

Bamboo has a variety of claims. One is that it is a grass, and for centuries it has been classified as an invasive grass species. However, more recent investigations have begun to claim that the DNA is not indicative of a grass but rather of a plant. I maintain that it is a grass and will treat it as such since I have had the pleasure and pain of growing it around houses I have lived in and owned. The plant is amazingly strong and will get through anything. Years ago I was at the Royal Botanic Gardens at Kew in their bamboo garden. The giant bamboo shoots actually separated quarter-inch welded steel plating to come up in the middle of the nobedan path.

One does not "turn" bamboo. There isn't enough to actually work on a lathe. When making fishing rods and flooring the woody portion is shaved and shaped in layers. It may also be steamed, similar to other "green" woods that haven't dried out yet. When making a wand from bamboo, simply cut the length you need from enclosed node to enclosed node and then work it as you see fit. The walls are thin if you are using the end tips but once you get down to the larger pieces you might actually be able to get a solid piece of bamboo and hand-form it. If you can find a large enough piece and turn it roughly round, then you can work the wand with sandpaper on a very slow-moving lathe and get a very good result.

In legends the Filipinos believe that a man and a woman were created by coming forth from a bamboo stalk. Feats of cunning and bravery are also attributed to the bamboo, and the Japanese martial arts of kendo, kyudo, and karate all use bamboo as either training weapons or functional ones.

Magically the wand is great for construction, specifically high-rise office buildings. This is from the millennia of use as a scaffolding material throughout the East. Fishing rituals also benefit from the bamboo wand since it has been used as netting and cages for centuries. Also, high-end fly rods are made from bamboo, and if you fly-fish, then you should have

a bamboo wand. Even better if it's made from one of your broken rods for increased success in the lakes and streams.

Another use of the bamboo is for annoyance rituals. Cast a circle with a bamboo wand and send the energy of the grasses to those you wish to annoy. Depending on what annoyance you cast you can bring great misfortune to those who have harmed you. However, whatever you send out will return to you threefold, so be aware of the consequences of your actions.

Fig (Common)

ORDER: *Rosales*

FAMILY: *Moraceae*

GENUS: *Ficus*

SPECIES: *carica*

JANKA: 770

ENERGY: Masculine

ELEMENT(S): Fire

GOD(S) REPRESENTED: Jupiter, Dionysus

GODDESS(ES) REPRESENTED: Juno, Isis

Most figs are either brown turkey figs or black figs. The brown turkey fig is the most prominent in the United States at the moment, although the black fig is being sold in more nurseries and larger lumberyards. It is a hardy tree and will grow well anywhere the temperature stays above 5 degrees Fahrenheit; therefore, you won't find many of these in the northern states, where the temperature dips into the single or low double digits regularly. Also, if the ground has a long freeze or frost the plant will die. The tree does very well in dry or semidry areas, but it needs a water source. The roots are invasive and send out long tendrils to find water if no standing or running water is readily available.

In the Bible Adam and Eve are said to cover themselves with fig leaves after they eat of the forbidden fruit. The fig leaf is therefore associated with guilt and shame, and during many reigns throughout English and some European monarchies fig leaves were used to cover up the genitals of statues rather than embarrass or shock the monarchs on the throne. During Victorian times many museums had portable fig leaves ready to cover statue genitals in the event that Victoria came through on one of her visits.

Since the tree grows quickly, the fig is a good source of wand wood as well as other smaller projects. The wood is clear with few grain lines and turns easily with common lathe tools. When shaping the wand, much of the work after cutting out the blank may be done with a 40 coarse sandpaper and takes finer grains well.

The fig wand is particularly good for protection. With the wand in a standard grip, a protection spell or ritual may be performed with solid grounding and a relative degree of success. In conjunction with other talismans or sigils the wand will cast a solid spell for the user. The wand is also very good for casting love spells. If you are trying to conceive, the fertility spell you cast should be performed with a fig wand instead of the many others available.

Since the fig has historically been used for coverage, another good spell for this wood is invisibility. If you wish to disappear from sight, either by blending into your surroundings or dropping off the grid, this is the wood for you. The fig will give you a good coverage and allow you to slip away; however, you need to make certain that in your spell you add something about staying safe and with the ability to return when desired. Some spells may be written and performed in such a way that they are one-way, and that is not always a good thing.

Finally, the fig is used for safety in travel. Cunningham says in his *Encyclopedia of Magical Herbs*, that if you place a fig branch across your front door when you leave on a trip, you will return safely; therefore, using a fig wand for a safety travel spell is an excellent choice. You may use the wand to power the fig branch for added safety in your travels.

Lavender

ORDER: *Lamiales*

FAMILY: *Lamiaceae*

GENUS: *Lavandula*

SPECIES: *angustifolia*

JANKA: N/A

ENERGY: Masculine

ELEMENT(S): Air

GOD(S) REPRESENTED: Mercury, Sucellus

GODDESS(ES) REPRESENTED: Cybele, Hegemone

Lavender is a member of the mint family and very similar in structure to rosemary. It is an aromatic shrub that can get quite woody at the central stalk and therefore makes a good wand, albeit it must be worked by hand. Commercially it is grown for its aromatic purposes and for its oils which are used in perfumes and home sprays. When I was growing up, my father taught guitar in our home, and many of his students would give him colognes and sprays. Surprisingly, many of them were lavender. My mother would use the colognes in the toilet to make the bathroom smell better. To this day I cannot smell lavender without getting sick to my stomach due to the excess in that bathroom.

Medicinally the oils are good for antiseptic and anti-inflammatory uses. Bath salts have used lavender for centuries. During the First World War, lavender was used in hospitals as an antiseptic and to soothe soldiers' wounds. Care, however, should be taken when using lavender, since it is cytotoxic and could cause complications in women who are pregnant or nursing. Even though the flowers are used in cooking, be cautious whom you serve lavender to. There are many who have allergic reactions to the oils. Likewise, there are many who are now infusing lavender into cooking oils such as olive and almond. Ask before serving.

The wood in the stem is best worked by hand. Like rosemary, lavender wood is veined and heavily colored and gives a wonderful look to a wand, although the chances of making a straight one are limited. When crafting a lavender wand, accept the fact that the wand will be curved and natural in its appearance and go with it. Like many other woods in this section, the wand will do as it wishes, and you are merely the craftsperson who will bring out the form already chosen by the wood.

Magically the wood is good for protecting women's chastity while at the same time causing men to be attracted to women. I know that sounds like a no-win situation. The wand should be used to attract true love, and a circle with lavender burning in the brazier and a wand of lavender used to perform the attraction spell will go far to bring true love to you quickly.

The wand is also good for cleansing and purification. Use the bough to sweep away unwanted negativity in the spring and then burn the bough in your Beltane fire. This will keep your house and hearth safe throughout the year.

Finally, if you truly need something essential, lavender is excellent. Cast your circle with your lavender wand. Then with the green sprigs in your right hand and your wand in your left, walk the circle clockwise thrice beginning at north and reciting

> Three times I walk in time of need.
> Three times I ask but not for greed.
> Three times I ask for that I desire.
> Three times I feed this to the fire.

At each rotation of north place one-third of the needles into the brazier on the north quarter altar. At the last rotation stop at north and burn the last of the lavender, saying

> I have asked three times for that I need.
> I have asked three times but not from greed.
> I have asked three times for my desire.
> I have burned three times the sprigs in fire.

You should receive what you need within a fortnight if the Gods accept your petition.

Licorice Root

ORDER: *Fabales*

FAMILY: *Fabaceae*

GENUS: *Glycyrrhiza*

SPECIES: *glabra*

JANKA: N/A

ENERGY: Feminine

ELEMENT(S): Water

GOD(S) REPRESENTED:
Atepomarus, Lenus

GODDESS(ES) REPRESENTED: Venus

Licorice root is probably not something you would think of when creating a wand. The root is long but not all that straight at best, and it isn't thick enough to put on a lathe. However, the root is very workable as a hardened vascular wood and sands well by hand. Further, it is available thick enough to be a good-sized wand equal with many of the other woods that are described in this book.

The root contains both a heavy sweetening agent, many times stronger and sweeter than sugars, and a flavoring that is likened to anise. In fact, many of the candies that are sold as black licorice are augmented with anise seed oil to enhance the licorice flavor that we associate with the root.

Medicinally the root is good for stomach issues as well as issues of the mouth. Further, licorice has been linked with relief from irritable bowel syndrome and Crohn's disease since it assists in calming the bowels. Alternatively, the Chinese use the licorice for mouth ulcers and sores.

Did you know that almost 90 percent of all tobacco products have some form of licorice in them? The licorice supposedly enhances the experience of smoking. I find this fascinating and somewhat understandable, since chewing on licorice root is a way of naturally weaning yourself off smoking.

In any case, too much of a good thing is not a good thing. Eating or ingesting too much licorice may lead to severe muscle weakness and high blood pressure. Therefore, excessive use of the root or its end products is strongly discouraged.

Magically the root is a great wand for smoking cessation rituals. Just as long as you don't start chewing on your wand, you may use it in circle to heal smoking damage or inhibit the urge for the habit. Cast your circle with burned tobacco at south, captured tobacco smoke at east, chewed tobacco at west, and fresh leaf at north. Ask the Deities of the quarters for the strength to resist the damaging habit of smoking or chewing tobacco and then cast your habit to the winds to be borne away from you. After you have taken down the circle, bury the tobacco products from the ritual by your front door or the door you use the most. That will give you residual protection against the prior effects of the habit and renewed strength to keep from starting the habit again.

Poison Ivy

ORDER: *Sapindales*

FAMILY: *Anacardiaceae*

GENUS: *Toxicodendron*

SPECIES: *radicans*

JANKA: N/A

ENERGY: Feminine

ELEMENT(S): Earth, Fire

CELTIC OGHAM: Gort

GOD(S) REPRESENTED: Pluto, Ra, Thoth

GODDESS(ES) REPRESENTED: Hel

Poison ivy is not a plant that one would immediately think of as a wand choice. The fact that the plant is highly toxic, hence the common name poison, and the fact that it's not an ivy, make it a poisonous liar. However, this vine is quite possible for a wand, although not for the reasons you may think. As witches we like to think that we practice positive magic and employ the positive energies of the cosmos. Poison ivy is the antithesis of everything we teach as witches. It is the ultimate dark magic wand, dripping in poison that could ultimately kill the user if he or she is susceptible to its oils and saps. But I won't only offer the light and fluffy half of magic wands. There must be balance in all things, because without light there can be no dark, and vice versa.

Poison ivy is dangerous due to urushiol, the clear liquid that the plant produces within the sap. Once this sap is released, it can remain toxic for days, months, or even years, thus causing the plant to be avoided at all costs. Another common name for this is *Rhus radicans*, and that is how I learned it as a landscape architect. This plant may be found throughout North America, mostly in forested areas or areas that have been cleared. It does very well as a ground cover, unfortunately for many, and it will climb trees as a vine, often reaching a thickness of over a few inches.

There are many myths about poison ivy. One is that you can spread it by scratching the sores and transfering the liquid, which is plasma, to other sections of your skin. That is supposedly proven because you get poison ivy later on different areas. In fact, you get poison ivy at different times because some skin cells are denser than others and some oils come in contact with you at different times. Once you have poison ivy and have completely washed with a cleansing soap, you are pretty much safe. I am deathly allergic to poison ivy and live with it in my blood. When I bruise severely, I get the rash from subcutaneous bleeding, which is what a bruise is. When I get poison ivy, I scratch it with a stiff brush till it bleeds and then I pour isopropyl alcohol over the open sore. Not pretty and not pleasant, but I guarantee it stops the itch.

Another myth is that you can pass poison ivy on to someone else. That is both true and false. If you have the oil on your skin or clothes, then you are contagious. If you already have the rash but are clear of the oil, then you are safe to be around. Also, avoid the dead leaves and smoke of the burning plant. Both will transmit the oils as microscopic particles.

Poison ivy is a dark magic plant. There is no light to this wand. Unlike black walnut or ebony, which may be used for both positive and negative magic, poison ivy is purely dark. Any spell cast with a poison ivy wand will be a negative spell, and no amount of wishing or hoping will make the wand work as a positive wand. Therefore, and this is where I include wands of both forces, you should be very careful when you harvest a poison ivy wand blank, fashion a wand, and employ that wand for magical purposes. There are some things in this universe that should not be used or done, but a warning is all you get at this point. The ultimate decision is yours.

No examples of spells or rituals are offered for this wand.

Rosemary

ORDER: *Lamiales*

FAMILY: *Lamiaceae*

GENUS: *Rosmarinus*

SPECIES: *officinalis*

JANKA: N/A

ENERGY: Masculine

ELEMENT(S): Fire

GOD(S) REPRESENTED: Vulcan

GODDESS(ES) REPRESENTED: Aphrodite

Rosemary is a shrub of not sizeable proportions, so you are probably wondering why it is included in a wand book. The answer is that the central stakes and shoots of the plant are quite large enough to turn or carve into a useable wand.

Rosemary is a surprisingly hard wood for being an evergreen. It seldom grows larger than a shrub with long branches and many finer ones. The greenery remains throughout the year, and the plant does well in dry areas as long as there is dew or mist to keep the needles moist. Many nurseries recommend that rosemary be planted near your front door, and I concur with that assessment.

When planting rosemary, remember that the shrub does not appreciate wet feet. Similar to the arborvitae, another evergreen shrub, the soil around the rosemary may be moist or damp but not continually wet or flooded. Further, some varieties are very prone to severe frost damage, so close to the house is in more ways than one a good position for this shrub.

Magically the rosemary has been used for many things: oils, potions, rituals, and more. Legend has it that Aphrodite covered herself in it when she rose fully grown from the sea, and the Virgin Mary covered a rosemary with her cloak and that's why the white flowers are now also sometimes blue.

In traditional medicine rosemary has been used for centuries as a tonic to revitalize the limbs and joints. This tonic was first prepared for Elizabeth of Hungary in the late fourteenth century. Rosemary was mixed with strong brandy and used to regenerate the queen. It is also credited with assisting the memory and is used at weddings and funerals. Humorously enough, rosemary was also thought to repel witches and was planted around castles and keeps in the Middle Ages. So much for that.

In ritual rosemary may be used for protection, and not necessarily from just witches. Placing sprigs of rosemary at the four quarters of your circle will ensure that you will be extra safe during your ritual. Afterward, keep the rosemary safe until the next circle and then burn that as your protective incense in the ritual fire while thanking the Deities for their support. Students would do well to use rosemary sachets when studying for exams and when preparing oral presentations. The rosemary will aid one's memory and help with recalling specific answers to questions.

A wand of rosemary is very powerful for evoking scholarly accomplishments, and with the sprigs at the four quarters, some burning in the brazier, and the wand in your hand, your circle should be quite powerful and enough to propel you to an exceptional grade or performance. Actors and others that require memory for their livelihood would be well served with a rosemary wand in their toolbox.

Wisteria (American)

ORDER: *Fabales*

FAMILY: *Fabaceae*

GENUS: *Wisteria*

SPECIES: *frutescens*

JANKA: N/A

ENERGY: Feminine

ELEMENT(S): Air

GOD(S) REPRESENTED: A'as, Ganesha, Prometheus

GODDESS(ES) REPRESENTED: Mary

Most of us have admired the wisteria growing along fences or cascading from tall trees in the American Southeast. The large purple blooms give early color to the countryside, and with the dogwood and the magnolia it cries out southern charm and gentility. However, the vine is also found throughout the Far East, where it is a native plant used in many celebrations and festivals.

When making a wand of wisteria, you have a number of choices. The smaller branches may be hand-formed and the larger trunk—many wisterias will grow to a foot across at the base—may be turned unconventionally on a lathe. Either way, work the wood with reverence since it is a softer wood than the hard and semihard trees you may be used to. Since the wood is so soft, you cannot use tools on the lathe. Even if the tools are razor-sharp, the vine will snap. Therefore, you will get much better results if you just start with a rough 40 grit sandpaper and work your way down from there. It didn't take me long to shape a wand with sandpaper, but you have to take breaks occasionally because the vibrations of using sandpaper on corners of the blank will cause your hands to go numb.

Magically wisteria is good for clarity and learning. According to some early witches this wood has been used to gain positive energies by inhaling the fragrances and then pursuing one's endeavors. A tea from the flower is also good for the brain and critical thinking. A circle cast with a wisteria wand will condense the energies to the one casting the circle and give that person the power to see through the cloud to what is actually out there and what is important to the task at hand.

With the wand in your heart hand (left), cast the circle as tightly as possible around you without being constrictive. Then, with the energies of the wisteria bound by the tight circle, sit comfortably in the center and with the wand laying across your lap, head pointed to the east, concentrate on what you would like to discover or perceive. Once you have completed your meditation, dismiss the circle by grounding the energy and casting the boundary of the circle upward. This will make certain that all residual energy is put back into the earth and the wards are safely out of the way in the Aether.

Broadleaf Evergreens

Broadleaf evergreens are curious plants. They are by name broad-leafed but do not lose or drop their leaves during times of cold or heat. However, they are also not cold tolerant and therefore are often missing in the northern climates that are so popular with the deciduous broadleaf and coniferous evergreens. While most of these plants are grown as either decorative flowering plants or shrubs, some of them may become quite tall, stately, and take on the tree form they truly are. Examples of a shrub growing into a tree include hollies and some of the magnolias.

When looking for wand material, the tree is going to give you a larger, straighter, and more structurally sound piece of material by virtue of its age and thickness. However, if you are going to create a wand by hand, which is the way many of our students are required to make their wands, then any piece that is large enough to fit the requirements of a wand may in fact become a wand.

Bay

ORDER: *Laurales*

FAMILY: *Lauraceae*

GENUS: *Laurus*

SPECIES: *nobilis*

JANKA: 1270

ENERGY: Masculine

ELEMENT(S): Fire

GOD(S) REPRESENTED: Apollo, Eros

GODDESS(ES) REPRESENTED: Ceres

Bay is also commonly known as bay laurel, although most who purchase bay candles and bay leaves buy them for the name bay and nothing else. This laurel may grow quite large and quite broad in mature specimens. The tree is a broadleaf evergreen, although the leaves are not as broad as one might think if considering magnolias in the same classification. The tree is most characteristically used for its leaves in cooking and as a spice for foods. However, the oils in the flowers are often used by massage therapists and as an astringent for poison ivy and other skin conditions.

I love turning bay. The shop smells for days after the process, and the wood is a joy to work with *if* you let it dry. Bay is extremely moist and cracks as it dries. Therefore, you must pick and choose how you cut your pieces to avoid splits and weak areas. Also, if you turn the wood damp or green, it bounces excessively, making a smooth turn difficult. A dry piece of bay, though, will turn well and sand smooth with a slight gray pattern running the length of the wand. It's one of the ways you can tell a bay wand from a number of other light-colored wands without smelling it.

Magically a bay wand is very good as a defense against the darker magic employed by the poison ivy wand. The leaves may also be burned in a brazier to assist in the identification of those who are attempting to do you harm, and a visioning spell should be called up and used in this situation.

This is why bay is a good choice for a hearth wand when you are looking for one for your home.

The wand may also be used as a health and healing wand for those with arthritis, melanoma, or skin allergies. Direct the wand at the afflicted area while concentrating your energies or those of your group/coven/airship. Envision the area clearing up and healing quickly and without side effects or long-term damage.

Other magical uses may be in potions that need additional resources or powers. A few bay leaves in the mix and a specially turned bay wand to be used as a stirring rod will infuse all the power that you require into the liquid or gel.

Holly

ORDER: *Aquifoliales*

FAMILY: *Aquifoliaceae*

GENUS: *Ilex*

SPECIES: *aquifolium*

JANKA: 1860

ENERGY: Masculine

ELEMENT(S): Earth, Air, Fire

CELTIC OGHAM: Tinne

GOD(S) REPRESENTED: Frey, Tyr, Saturn, Ares

GODDESS(ES) REPRESENTED: Gaia, Danu

The holly that grows in your hedge and reaches maybe eight feet if you leave it untended and the holly that grows in your backyard and becomes a one-hundred-foot tree, although both *Ilex*, are significantly different in characteristics and properties. The shrub version of the holly is difficult to grow or find a piece large enough for a wand. It is a shrub and therefore is forked, short-stemmed, and grows in spurts. The holly that you want for wands is the English holly or common holly (*Ilex aquifolium*) that grows to substantial heights and produces straight and relatively strong branching.

Both hollies are difficult to turn on a lathe, and if you do not have the patience or skills necessary to turn a very soft and bouncy piece of wood, then you would be better off forming this wand by hand. On a lathe you will get long, almost pencil sharpener–length pieces of wood that are delicate and well formed. Don't let that fool you. The wood is very pliable at the ½- to ³/₈-inch diameter and will catch on your chisel and snap.

In mythology, the Holly King is said to rule over the land for the winter half of the year, and the Oak King rules during the summer half. During Christmastime the holly became the shrub of choice for its similarity to the crown of thorns of Christ, as demonstrated by the sharp pointed leaves, and the blood-red berries, for the blood. However, if you look at the myth and the tradition you will find that the practice of using holly during the Yule season predates the Christian myths in many cultures.

In the Celtic tradition the holly is represented by the eighth letter called *Tinne*. It is said that the powdered leaves, when made into a tea, would cure measles, although time will do that too, and breathing the smoke of the leaves would alleviate whooping cough. For all the medicinal purposes of the leaves, the berries are quite poisonous to young children, and in adults they will cause nausea and severe sickness.

Holly is also the antithesis to ebony. Where one is one of the darkest woods in the world, the other is one of, if not the, whitest. Holly wands are known for their purity, their strength of spells, and their protection of their user. A holly wand should be turned at the height of the full moon, preferably with the moon shining down on your tools, although other lighting may be required for safety.

Holly, when used in ritual, is a sensitive wood and will not respond to its user if his or her intentions are not pure and right. While some dark magic may be performed with other woods, ebony and black walnut being two, it is impossible to perform dark magic with a holly wand. The wand itself will just not allow you to do anything untoward. For this reason many dark witches and magicians choose not to use the holly wand or have a piece of holly in their magical space since the vibrations of the wood will oftentimes negate other wands and spells.

It is interesting that this wood, among so many others in this list, was planted to keep witches from entering one's home. This is curious since the same wood was used for the solstice, referred to by the Romans as Saturnalia, and hung as a decoration. I imagine that to one culture witches were something to be protected against, while in a different culture at the same time they were used for acceptance.

Laurel (English)

ORDER: *Rosales*

FAMILY: *Rosaceae*

GENUS: *Prunus*

SPECIES: *laurocerasus*

JANKA: 1790

ENERGY: Masculine

ELEMENT(S): Air, Fire

GOD(S) REPRESENTED: Apollo, Baldur

GODDESS(ES) REPRESENTED: Ceres

Laurels are popular throughout most of the United States as ornamental evergreen shrubs. The plant grows to a moderate height and covers well, although it can get spindly when allowed to grow wild. Close cropping is necessary to keep the shrub cut back and viable. The English laurel is not to be confused with "true" laurel, the *Laurus nobilis*, nor is it close to the cherry laurel (*Prunus caroliniana*), even though they are in the same genus.

The wood is hard to turn but does not fight you on the lathe. Fortunately for wood turners, the stems grow relatively straight, and therefore wand blanks are possible without resorting to hand-crafting your pieces with curve in them like some of the smaller shrubs and vines. Care should be used when dealing with anything other than the wood, since the seeds of the fruit contain a cyanogenic that will cause stomach distress if consumed.

In mythology the laurel was the nymph Daphne whom Apollo fell in love with after an arrow by Eros. Daphne did not love Apollo nor the attention, so she escaped to the river of her father, Paneus. Desperate to save his daughter, Paneus turned Daphne into a laurel. Grief-stricken Apollo then turned the laurel into an evergreen so that her leaves would never dry up and fall.

The laurel is a good wand to use for creativity and divination. For creativity, cast a circle with your wand and burn some dried laurel leaves in the brazier on your altar. With the smoke swirling about you, cast out into the Aether or the Void as you wish and bring back your ideas as concrete thoughts and plans. This ritual will solidify what you have been trying to tie down, so to speak, in your mind, and you will be able to get on with your plans successfully and with great zeal.

For divination, place a single laurel leaf in your brazier in a small, quiet space, and with your wand pointing north look into the future, or if you wish, the past, and clearly identify what you need to know or that you need to find the one you need to ask your question to. With the smoke of the laurel leaf you will be able to navigate the expanse in front of you, and with your wand pointing the way you will get out into the expanse safely. By following the base back to your starting point, you will be able to return with the answers you were needing or wanting (which are not always the same thing).

Magnolia (Southern)

ORDER: *Magnoliales*

FAMILY: *Magnoliaceae*

GENUS: *Magnolia*

SPECIES: *grandiflora*

JANKA: 1020

ENERGY: Feminine

ELEMENT(S): Water

GOD(S) REPRESENTED: Jord

GODDESS(ES) REPRESENTED: Goguryeo

The magnolia is an amazing old and large genus. Botanists believe that the flowers of the magnolia predate bee pollination and that they evolved to allow beetles to do the job instead. In that there is such variety in the genera I shall speak of two of the most common magnolias: the southern magnolia (*Magnolia grandiflora*) and the hybrid saucer magnolia (*Magnolia x soulangeana*).

The standard *grandiflora* magnolia is the one you see in yards and parks throughout the South. It is the magnolia that usually comes to mind when you think of the songs of the South or scenery in southern movies. The fragrance of the magnolia in the summertime will often overpower every other scent in the area, and more than a few country songs have mentioned the flower or the tree.

The *soulangeana* is an early blooming hybrid from the eighteenth century. The blooms are large and preempt the leaves, which is why the small trees are used as decorative plantings in yards and gardens. The saucer magnolia is also referred to as the Japanese magnolia, even though it has no relation to that region geographically or botanically.

The wood of the magnolia is clear, and the *grandiflora* grows to such a size that timber is possible for larger projects. It is easy to turn the wood if it is wet or damp and then sand it once it's dry; however, it is also very easy to turn the wood dry.

Medicinally the tree has limited uses other than for aromatherapy. The Chinese variety, called the cucumber magnolia, or *Magnolia acuminata*, found throughout the colder regions of the central eastern United States was originally used to treat malaria in China. The bark has a substance similar to quinine and is part of the Chinese regimen of herbs and spices.

Magically the wand of a magnolia is very good for southern heritage magic. While not necessarily root magic, southern heritage magic is best described as upper-class, genteel white magic. This is in contrast to the root conjure magic of Appalachia, where the magicians are closer to the soil. A minor distinction, but one worthy of comment.

Another very good use of this wand is core earth magic. The tree is so old and so tied to the earth that this is an excellent wand to work with Gaia and the spirits of the ancient earth.

Witch Hazel (Chinese)

ORDER: *Saxifragales*

FAMILY: *Hamamelidaceae*

GENUS: *Loropetalum*

SPECIES: *chinense*

JANKA: N/A

ENERGY: Feminine

ELEMENT(S): Fire

GOD(S) REPRESENTED:
  Wong Tai Sin

GODDESS(ES) REPRESENTED:
  Sekhmet, Serket, Tai Bitjet

Although the *Loropetalum* is not the common American witch hazel, which is the *Hamamelis virginiana*, it is a witch hazel nonetheless. This is the witch hazel that you see mostly in the Southeast, and the campuses of the Carolinas are filled with its hot-pink blooms in spring. The tree—or shrub, depending on how you plant and trim it—will do very well in temperate to slightly colder climates, and it survives into the twenty-degree areas, although if it gets much colder than that the shrub may die back to the root and the main stalk and not survive. As a broadleaf evergreen it is susceptible to extreme cold.

Similar to other shrubs, this plant is soft and turns easily if you are careful. The wood tends to bounce, so care is always recommended. Also, the oils in the wood are witch hazel in nature. If you work the wood bare-handed be very careful to keep your fingers away from your eyes. Also, when sanding the wood after it dries, I recommend having a fan behind you to keep the dust off your skin, lest you know the joys of medicinal coolness. In other words, if you don't want to feel or smell as though you just came through an alcohol rub, then you might want to be extra cautious.

Magically this variety of witch hazel is still good for the oils that make up the witch hazel that can be purchased over the counter for sores and other bruises and pains. The oil is also very good for acne and other oily skin problems and will cool you off if you use a little during the extreme heat of the summer.

A wand of *Loropetalum* will cast a circle or spell that will ease sore muscles and, with proper nutrition and therapy, resolve pulled or torn ligaments. The wand is best stored near a poison ivy wand if you are concerned about your ivy wand casting negative energy throughout your altar or storage area. The astringent in the oil of the *Loropetalum* is good for treatment of poison ivy and is an excellent positive magic defense against anyone wielding a poison ivy wand against you. Other rituals that the wand would be appropriate for include healing rituals after childbirth.

Coniferous Trees

Coniferous trees are identifiable in two ways: First, they produce a cone. Second, the needles on the branches are long and slender, unlike leaves on either the deciduous or broadleaf trees and shrubs. The coniferous evergreens are found into the very coldest of climates as well as in the tropical climates of the Deep South. They are unique in that the resin forms amber when petrified. Further, some of the species have developed resistance to many tree fungals and insects and a very few secrete a fire-retardant material that allows them to be burned in grass fires without severe damage.

Unlike the oaks, the pines of this group are very similar when turned. They all are of a general white or light yellow–colored nature with a darkened heart and large, open grain. They are heavily knotted as well from the multiple levels of branches and therefore may be problematic when put on a lathe. With that, many of the lighter pine and other coniferous wands would be better crafted by hand or lighter hand tools. However, that is up to the skill of the craftsperson working the wood.

Cedar (Deodar)

ORDER: *Pinales*

FAMILY: *Pinaceae*

GENUS: *Cedrus*

SPECIES: *deodara*

JANKA: 600

ENERGY: Masculine

ELEMENT(S): Earth, Air, Fire, Water

GOD(S) REPRESENTED: Osiris, Ra, Shiva

GODDESS(ES) REPRESENTED: Lakshmi, Sita

Cedar has been used as a repellant of insects as well as a building wood for many thousands of years. The deodar is a most holy cedar, however, because of its ties to the Hindu religion and religious leaders of India and Pakistan. This is a large and tall tree, sometimes growing to a height of 180 feet with a trunk in excess of 10 feet. The wood is heavily grained and darkened at the inner rings, giving it a beautiful appearance when used for furniture and other building pieces such as temples. The name *deodar* comes from two Sanskrit words meaning "wood of the god." To that end, the deodar is a favorite material for temple furniture and structures and is used to build houses for the Gods within the temples. These temples are often built within forests or stands of deodar to enhance the connectivity between Shiva and his priests.

Medicinally the bark as well as other pieces of the tree have been used holistically for hundreds of years. The wood is used for aromatics and is good for breathing. The oil pressed from the tree is used as an insect repellant for both animals and humans and is a strong antifungal medicine when used directly. The oil today is used in a wide array of household products from perfumes to cleaning liquids to soaps.

Magically the deodar cedar wand is exceptional for meditation. Cast your circle with the deodar wand, and while burning a small candle and some cedar chips in a brazier in front of you, seek what it is that you wish to know. Be very specific in your question, because the wand and the wood chips give you a direct line to your God/dess, and as in all other situations the God/dess is busy. Do not take up valuable time fumbling with a query.

The wand is also good for healing. If there is a sick or injured individual in your coven, cast your circle with the wand and then, using the wand as a pointer, begin at the heart of the person as he or she is lying on the ground and radiate outward in a clockwise manner. Once you have reached the toes of the individual, reverse the process until you are again at his or her heart. At the heart conclude your ritual. The person should feel better soon.

Cedar (Eastern Red)

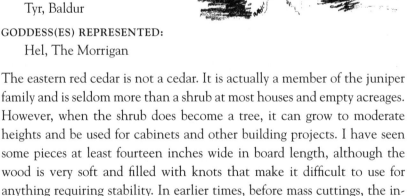

ORDER: *Pinales*

FAMILY: *Cupressaceae*

GENUS: *Juniperus*

SPECIES: *virginiana*

JANKA: 900

ENERGY: Masculine

ELEMENT(S): Earth, Fire

GOD(S) REPRESENTED: Loki,
Tyr, Baldur

GODDESS(ES) REPRESENTED:
Hel, The Morrigan

The eastern red cedar is not a cedar. It is actually a member of the juniper family and is seldom more than a shrub at most houses and empty acreages. However, when the shrub does become a tree, it can grow to moderate heights and be used for cabinets and other building projects. I have seen some pieces at least fourteen inches wide in board length, although the wood is very soft and filled with knots that make it difficult to use for anything requiring stability. In earlier times, before mass cuttings, the indigenous peoples of the Pacific Northwest often made their canoes from red cedar, sometimes as long as sixty feet, but now the trees are hard to find at that size. Missouri currently claims the oldest red cedar, at over seven hundred years old.

Red cedar pollen is a serious respiratory complaint in the Texas Hill Country, as well as other areas where strong winds carry large amounts of dust or pollen. The cedar dust settles on everything, and those who have breathing problems from allergies and sinus conditions during the pollen season suffer greatly. I had a professor as a graduate student who hated going home to Austin during the red cedar pollen season because when he would return, even after just a weekend visit, his eyes would be puffy, his breathing short, and his nose plugged up. Even as far north as the central portion of Oklahoma the pollen was evident, and those with severe allergies suffered greatly during that time of year.

Turning wands of red cedar is difficult at best. The wood is very, very soft and breaks easily, and this is backed up by the Janka placement of the very lower third on the scale. There are few pieces that are clear enough to give a knot-free wand blank, and once the blank is cut, even if the wood is very dry and cured, it will still have a tendency to warp badly. Add this to the fact that the wood is dry and subject to cracking and it's no surprise that the wands are hard to find and keep.

If you choose to pursue having a red cedar wand, make certain to take extra precautions and cover your nose and throat from the dust coming off the wand as you sand it. The red cedar wand I have in my collection is coated with Scott's Liquid Gold, and I keep the wand hydrated with the preservative constantly.

Spell work with red cedar, though, is very good. The wood is aromatic and therefore good for healing, even though the pollen is hard on the lungs in large amounts. Red cedar is used for closets and as sachets to keep destructive insects out of your clothing, especially your wools and linens, and therefore it is very valuable as a wand for protection. In the late winter and early spring, when the pollen is most prevalent, a spell cast with a red cedar wand will draw additional energy from any pollen-laden air around you, and even though you may not breathe as well as you did during the clear summer or crisp fall months, the spell will have added force and therefore work better for you.

Money spells are also very effective with red cedar. Money draw incenses are mixed with red cedar to add potency to the spells, and you may use that in conjunction with your wand for additional effect. Since red cedar is a juniper, you may also use gin if you use alcohol in your spells or rituals. The gin derives its strong flavor from juniper berries, and in fact the word *gin* is either from French or Dutch origin and both mean "juniper." The gin, along with the incense and the wand, will give you a very strong money spell and should work quite quickly.

Medically, the juniper is good for a number of ailments from colds to general pains. Using the oils from the plant, you may make a salve for topical application or you may brew the potion for internal use. However, be very careful of the dose and the parts used and consult an expert before attempting any potion work.

Cypress (Bald)

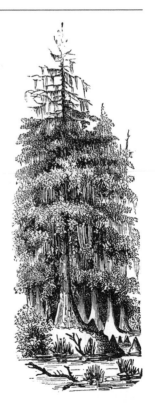

ORDER: *Pinales*

FAMILY: *Cupressaceae*

GENUS: *Taxodium*

SPECIES: *distichum*

JANKA: 570

ENERGY: Feminine

ELEMENT(S): Earth, Water

GOD(S) REPRESENTED: Osiris, Zeus, Jupiter

GODDESS(ES) REPRESENTED: Ashtoreth, Diana, Artemis

Cypress are some of the oldest trees in the United States, and although the bald cypress doesn't reach the ancientness of the redwoods of the Northwest, trees may still be found that are over fifteen hundred years old in the southeastern United States. The bald cypress is found in low-lying areas where there is a steady source of water. In fact, the growth of the tree is dictated by the amount of water available.

Cypress trees are noted for their knees that some legends say assist them in accessing air, specifically carbon dioxide, and the knees of some cypress, such as the ones around the cypress swamps of northern Florida, have knees that exceed four feet high. However, more recent research indicates that the knees assist in stabilization of the trees, which is a new theory that has been proposed recently due to an abundance of trees living where no standing water is evident. These knees, either low to the ground or high and almost treelike, cause problems for pedestrians, boaters, and other travelers. Because of their slow growth and our urban sprawl, it is doubtful that we will ever see another stand of cypress to the density and size of the ones cut in the early twentieth century in Florida.

When planting or calling out cypress, it is imperative to remember the size of the tree and the spread of the branches at full growth. I lived next door to a family in Oklahoma and both our backyards flooded badly due to poor drainage swales. I and the family to my north raised the land to be above the high waterline. My neighbor on the other side planted a bald cypress and a willow not more than ten feet apart. Within five years both trees were fighting for superiority; the cypress eventually won, and the yard was lost to fallen leaves in the autumn and shade that kept everything from growing. Unfortunately, the water never abated enough for the family to enjoy their backyard, and when I bought the house a few years later, I had to fill in the back third, as I did to my own, and then deal with the two quite large and competing trees.

Magically the cypress is an excellent tree for water work. If you need water, then a spell cast with a cypress wand will do much to assist you in producing rain for your crops or garden. Using the head of the wand as the projection end, cast the circle and then create your spell to specifically call out what water you need/want and where. It seldom does anyone any good to generally call for rain without a target or amount. You end up with events such as Hurricane Katrina.

You may also use the tail end as your projection end and perform a ritual and circle for water protection. If you are in fear of flood or heavy water damage, then a ritual to that effect will be quite useful. It is always necessary to provide other more structural items too, though, such as levees, dykes, or swales. In either case, water is your primary use for a cypress wand, although other rituals may be performed with it too.

A good friend of mine does mountain magic, also referred to as root magic. He is a conjurer, and a very good one at that. To that end he works with his ancestors and others who have come before him. The cypress, due to its longevity in the South, is a very good, if not perfect, wand for heritage work or conjure magic. The deep roots of the southern swamps, so indicative of the low-lying states of Louisiana, Alabama, Mississippi, and Georgia, almost demand a wand of that region. The cypress wands are perfect for those areas since the roots of the trees and the roots of the magic are one with the spirits of the land and the water.

The last use of cypress, and this may apply to cedar and juniper as well, is that the aroma or odor of the trees may be used to mask the smells of rotting bodies in cemeteries. That may be why in Europe you see cypress trees in such abundance around graveyards. A wand of cypress may be used to mask your "scent" if you are being sought by a wayward spirit or other manifestation. Burning cypress limbs while performing your protection ritual with a cypress wand will clear the way for your conquering the annoying spirit.

Cypress (Leyland)

ORDER: *Pinales*

FAMILY: *Cupressaceae*

GENUS: *Cupressus*

SPECIES: *leylandii*

JANKA: 430

ENERGY: Feminine

ELEMENT(S): Earth, Water

GOD(S) REPRESENTED: Osiris, Zeus, Jupiter

GODDESS(ES) REPRESENTED: Ashtoreth, Diana, Artemis

The Leyland cypress is more a shrub than a tree. At first glance it may appear to be an arborvitae, but if you look closer, you will see that the leaves are less flattened than the arbor. The trees grow quickly and become massive shrubs that can reach forty to fifty feet in height. In colder climates where there is a predominance of wind and possible snow, the Leyland makes a very good wind and snow break, although if allowed to reach full growth it may become invasive to neighbors.

The tree is a hybrid between the Monterey cypress and the Nootka cypress, two species indigenous to the United States. However, when placed in close proximity in a garden setting in England, the two mated and the new species, *leylandii* was created. Since the 1850s the Leyland has enjoyed success in a number of areas that other shrubs and trees could not.

Turning the Leyland is similar to turning other cypresses and true cedars. The wood is aromatic when being worked and sands well, although you must keep the wood oiled or otherwise sealed to keep it from drying out and featuring.

Magically the Leyland is very good for keeping things out or protection against large obstacles. The wand will draw energy from the surrounding landscape to protect the individual against overwhelming odds or overpowering forces. Further, if you use your wand in an offensive manner, you may be able to turn the tides of the force and repel it back to the one sending it to you.

While burning some dried sprigs of Leyland in a brazier, envision whom or what you are protecting yourself against. Then, as the smoke rises, hold your wand in your dominant hand with your arm outstretched in front of you and say three times

As these obstacles burn may the smoke return to those who sent them.

After the third refrain take your wand and wave it from the center of the smoke toward those who set the obstacles upon you, or if they are of natural occurrence, send them skyward. Your problems should be diminished soon after.

Fir (Douglas)

ORDER: *Pinales*

FAMILY: *Pinaceae*

GENUS: *Pseudotsuga*

SPECIES: *menziesii*

JANKA: 660

ENERGY: Masculine

ELEMENT(S): Air

CELTIC OGHAM: Ailm

GOD(S) REPRESENTED:
Pan, Osiris, Bacchus

GODDESS(ES) REPRESENTED: Diana, Isis, Artemis

The Douglas fir is not really a true fir. The Douglas fir is actually in the pine family but was classified as a fir in the late 1700s by the Scottish botanist and collector David Douglas, and the name stuck. It is the second-tallest cone-bearing tree in the world. The cones are distinct in that they are two-shaped, with wide, flat plates and smaller, sharper bracts. The trees are native to the northwestern United States and southwestern Canada, although they are also found as far south as Mexico in small stands and forests.

As a coniferous tree, it is a softwood and is prominently used as a building material since the wood is straight and clear-grained. Dimensional lumber and logs for log houses are most often cut from fir. The fir is often used as a Christmas tree and grown in large farms throughout the country for that purpose. Although able to reach a height in excess of four hundred feet with a trunk diameter of over twenty-five feet, most firs are now harvested and cut after a shorter life span to produce lumber and are then replanted.

Working with the Douglas fir is, as you might imagine, similar to any other soft cone-bearing tree. The wood is easy to turn and gives a good, although not excellent, finish with sandpaper. With any coniferous the sanding will take you only so far without sealing the wood in lacquer due to its open grain. However, the aging wood becomes exceptionally hard (though not as hard as fully dried hemlock).

There is a myth among the native peoples of the western United States that the bract that protrudes from the cone is actually the tail and two hind feet of a field mouse trying to avoid danger. The story goes like this: The field mouse lived his life in fear of capture by the wily fox. Day and night the mouse worried that the fox would catch and eat the small mouse, so the mouse kept up his guard relentlessly. One day the mouse was lax and the fox pounced. The mouse was able to run but found only the cone of the Douglas fir to hide in. Unfortunately, the cone was too small for the mouse, and his tail and back feet can be seen to this day as he hides from the fox.

The fresh tree tips of the Douglas fir may be used for tea or syrup. Prune fresh green tips from the trees and either steep in hot water or make a sun tea. You may also turn the tea into a syrup by straining it into a sauce-pan. Cook the tea with sugar until it has reduced to a syrup. The syrup will last a month or two refrigerated and is excellent on hotcakes or waffles.

Magically the Douglas fir is excellent for climbers or anyone who works with heights. The majesty of the tree translates its powers to any wands made from Douglas fir and will bring safety and success to those who are in the climbing or logging businesses. Also, those who work in the forests, such as park rangers and fish and game agents, should use a Douglas fir wand for safety during their work travels.

Hemlock

ORDER: *Pinales*

FAMILY: *Pinaceae*

GENUS: *Tsuga*

SPECIES: *spp*

JANKA: 500

ENERGY: Feminine

ELEMENT(S): Water

GOD(S) REPRESENTED: Alaunus, Dian Cecht

GODDESS(ES) REPRESENTED: Hecate

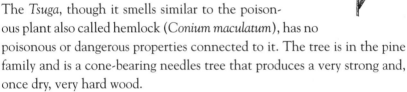

The *Tsuga*, though it smells similar to the poisonous plant also called hemlock (*Conium maculatum*), has no poisonous or dangerous properties connected to it. The tree is in the pine family and is a cone-bearing needles tree that produces a very strong and, once dry, very hard wood.

When Marla and I lived in New Hampshire, I built our first house. As a Yankee and a builder, I wanted to use native woods, but I wanted the house to stand against the elements. For six months I looked at all the old barns in the upper portion of the state to see what they were made of since they usually outlived their houses. The majority of the two-hundred-year-old structures were built with hemlock. So I built my house from locally cut and milled hemlock, and the wood, used wet, dried to a point where nails simply would not come out. Although I don't have the house anymore, I am certain that it will stand for another one hundred fifty to two hundred years in the same condition it was completed in.

Turning hemlock is fun. It is a soft wood, unless you find a very old and seasoned piece, at which point prepare for a battle. It's a little darker most times than pine and has a pleasant odor when being turned. As a softwood, it takes sandpaper well and smooths up to a good result.

There is a lengthy poem called *The Hemlock Tree and Its Legends* by Robert Bradbury, published in 1859. The poem is a response by the author to save an aged hemlock in Coopersville, New York, the tree being one of the author's favorites for contemplation and reflection. After talking to the owner of the tree, the plot of land was deeded to the author and after the author's death to the town. Such is the strength of the hemlock to elicit such a response. The poem is 113 pages long.

Magically the hemlock tree is important for healing and cleansing. Use a bough of the hemlock to sweep out your house during spring to cleanse the area, and in fall use the same dried bough to start your Yule fire since the dried boughs of hemlock are extremely flammable.

A wand turned from hemlock will give you a positive cleaning and healing spell. Cast your circle with the wand, and then using the wand, direct your energies—and anyone else's who may be in the circle with you—toward the one being healed. The concentrated energy of the wand will bring positive results.

Another trait of the hemlock is strength and determination. As I mentioned earlier, hemlock is a wood that dries hard and stays hard. Its strength is unmatched in softwoods. So is it with the wands of the wood. Your resolve and perseverance is enhanced by the use of this wand, and with it you should be able to accomplish many things that you probably thought impossible.

Pine

ORDER: *Pinales*

FAMILY: *Pinaceae*

GENUS: *Pinus*

SPECIES: *spp*

JANKA: 690

ENERGY: Masculine

ELEMENT(S): Air

GOD(S) REPRESENTED: Pan

GODDESS(ES) REPRESENTED: Astarte, Venus

Most of us have seen pine trees. We look at them in parks, forests, at lumberyards, when houses are being built, and when we buy cheap yard furniture. The pine is found throughout the world in all the temperate to colder climates of the Northern Hemisphere, and some species are even found close to the equator. They are identified by their thin needles in clusters and their cones, some large enough to fill a one- or two-quart dish singularly.

Pines are like oaks. Not in the sense that they are hard, which pine is not, but in the sense that there are two distinct groups of them and each has a specific use and a large selection of species. First is the yellow pine (*Pinus Pinus*), which is harder but more knotted. These are the pine boards you see in many lumberyards in the South. The wood is darker than the white pine and has a waxy or pitchy feeling to it even after being milled.

The white pine (*Pinus Strobus*) is clearer-grained, with fewer knots on the more select pieces, and much softer than its cousins. These are the pieces that are used for finish work in houses and other buildings and when toys are made of wood. The white pines make up an equal amount of distinctive varieties as the yellow, and it depends on what use you are looking for when choosing the wood. Further, the yellow pine is usually cheaper by the board foot.

Pine is an easy wood to turn. The white pine turns without incident and takes a good sanding. The yellow pine is a little more problematic since it feels brittle on the lathe and takes a less smooth sanding due to the nature of the wood. When choosing a pine for a lathe project, make certain that the wood is as clear of knots as possible since the knots of the pine are harder than many others once the wood has dried.

Pine nuts of some of the larger varieties are valued for their nutritional uses and may be found in many health food stores and other holistic venues. Further, the young needles of the tree are used as a tea in some Scandinavian countries since they are rich in vitamins A and C. Finally, a section of the bark may be dried and used as an additive with flour to make what the Native Americans refer to as bark bread.

In mythology the nymph Pitys was sought after by both Pan and Boreas. When she chose Pan, Boreas was so enraged he threw her off a ledge and killed her. When Pan found her lifeless body, he turned her into a pine tree, and that is why the sap, or tears of the pine, falls in the autumn when the north wind blows.

Magically the pine wand is used during fertility rituals as well as longevity ones. The wand is also very useful for protection of your house or home and may be implemented to cast a protective permeable bubble around your home to keep hardships and dangers away. Finally, you may use your pine wand for money spells. Begin a fire in your brazier with either a charcoal or piece of coal. Once the fire is started, throw in seven clusters of pine needles from a white pine and seven clusters of pine needles from a yellow pine. After the fire has burned out, take some of the ash and rub it on the front and back of a dollar bill. Carry that bill in your purse or wallet for good fortune, and money will come to you.

Spruce (Sitka)

ORDER: *Pinales*

FAMILY: *Pinaceae*

GENUS: *Picea*

SPECIES: *sitchensis*

JANKA: 510

ENERGY: Feminine

ELEMENTS: Earth, Water

GOD REPRESENTED: Poseidon

GODDESSES REPRESENTED: Cerridwen, Cybele

The sitka spruce is the fifth-largest coniferous in the plant kingdom, often growing over 240 feet tall. Some trees have grown over 300 feet tall in and around its namesake, Sitka, Alaska. The trees are found as far south as the Pacific Northwest and as far north as the Alaskan coast. Although the tree is a long-lived variety, it is also a fast grower so the overharvesting of some forests can be overturned with more careful management.

Like most other coniferous trees, the sitka spruce turns easily, and the redheart and inner wood have a similar appearance to its cousin the red cedar. It's hard for a coniferous, and the sitka is popular in instruments such as the piano, harp, guitar, and violin. The sitka, though, is even more important to the early aviation industry. The plane the Wright brothers flew at Kitty Hawk, North Carolina, was made partially of sitka spruce, as were the British Mosquito fighters' planes of World War I. Many of the Alaskan indigenous peoples use the bark of the sitka for baskets and other weavings, making the tree both economically important as well as culturally so.

Magically the sitka is perfect for flight safety, since the Wright brothers not only flew their plane but successfully landed it without incident. A wand turned of sitka spruce will give you solid results in safety rituals for any type of aviation, whether airplane or balloon. Also, the sitka may be employed by musicians to enhance their abilities through a ritual of the waxing moon. Cast a circle, call upon your particular Deities, and then with the sitka wand ask for increasing abilities culminating at the full moon. Remember to mention that after the full moon during the waning times your abilities should not diminish.

Yew

ORDER: *Pinales*

FAMILY: *Taxaceae*

GENUS: *Taxus*

SPECIES: *baccata*

JANKA: 1600

ENERGY: Masculine and Feminine

ELEMENT(S): Air, Fire, Water

CELTIC OGHAM: Idad

GOD(S) REPRESENTED: Hermes, Loki, Odin

GODDESS(ES) REPRESENTED: Hecate, Hel

The yew is an ancient tree with some specimens ranging from two to four thousand years old. The European yew, or common yew, is the one that most think about when they think yew because of its long history on the battlefield. It was the yew that made the English archers the scourge of war during the medieval times. The yew grows in such a way that it self-laminates, the inner core or heart of the tree resisting compression while the sapwood or outer layer of the stave resists stretching.

During the Hundred Years' War, the deciding Battle of Agincourt was fought with longbows. The English archers were outnumbered, but they had their yew bows, and the additional range that those bows could provide gave them the advantage over the French. Although the bows were not the only reason the English won the day, they were considerably important. At the end of the battle and after a few more major fights, Henry V was able to conquer the French. After that the English bowmen would put up their two bow fingers in a salute that they were able to defeat anyone they fired against. The two fingers, which became Winston Churchill's victory sign, were in defiance of the French, who would cut those two fingers off any archers they captured. Such was the fear of the French of the yew bow.

Working yew is fun. The wood is soft and turns easily, but the color is yellow to almost orange and the chips make a pleasant contrast to the whites and tans of most woods I turn. The wood, like many other harder evergreens, takes sandpaper well and oils to a high shine. The wood also avoids bouncing, possibly due to the nature of the grain or the fact that there are few knots in the wood that I use for wands. In either case, the wood won't fight you, and that makes all the difference.

Medicinally yew bark has been used for centuries as a cardiac remedy and calcium channel blocker. In the Himalayas the bark of the yew is used to treat ovarian and breast cancer. The bark is also used for the treatment of tuberculosis and some forms of arthritis, and there is a large-scale poaching operation in the western United States where the yew grows in large stands. Yew, however, is also toxic if taken in large enough doses. The

taxol derived from the bark is a high alkaloid and has historically been used as a poison.

Magically yew has been a choice of magical wands for hundreds of years. The druids of England are said to have used yew as well as oak for their wands, and Shakespeare chose yew for his three witches in *Macbeth*. For the Romans the yew was the third pillar of wisdom, along with oak and birch. Finally, the yew is important in dream weaving. Dreaming of a yew means that an older family member may die soon. If you dream you are sitting under a yew, that means you will die soon; but if you are instead admiring and complimenting the yew in your dream, you will live a long and full life.

Special Materials and Uses

Not all wands fit into neat little spaces. These previous pages have discussed woods that are easily understood, since they are the ones we work with in our yards, shops, circles, and hobbies. However, there are other aspects of wands that are less cut and dry but nonetheless important to us as magical users. The following three sections will look at woods that cannot be specifically defined by their genus or species.

Generational Wand

A generational wand begins with barnboard. Barnboard is actually not a genus or a species; it is a type of use, a generic listing of usually any type of wood, but most often coniferous for housing, and deciduous (usually oak) for storage such as barns. Barnboard became de rigueur in the late twentieth century as part of the primitive movement of construction and remodeling. The wood was pulled from many old and dilapidated barns and farmhouses to be resold to upscale contractors in remodeled Colonials.

The barnboard most useful for our purposes comes in pieces that are at least one hundred years old. There are still barns and farmhouses out there that are being restored, and many demolition companies have pieces of barnboard lying around that are either too damaged or too small to use for anything else but would make perfect wands.

Whenever I turn barnboard or make a box or other item with the wood, I always prepare myself for a fight. The wood, if it's coming from a floor—and especially a kitchen floor, where the heat from ovens has dried it for generations—is harder than some hardwoods. I would rather run a piece of sandy red oak through my planer than a clean piece of one-hundred-year-old barnboard. Further, I would rather turn a piece of yellowheart or maple, both relatively hard woods, than a piece of hardened pine from a South Carolina kitchen floor.

So why do we use barnboard if we can't tell what wood it is and it's a fight to even turn the piece? Because of its age. Barnboard is particularly good at generation work or rituals that involve ancestors or history. The ultimate would be to get a piece of your old house. The house that you grew up in. The house that perhaps one of your parents grew up in, too. I lived across the street from a couple in New Hampshire. When Eva was eighteen she married Harold. She was born in the house, and her parents gave it to her as a wedding gift. They moved, and Eva and Harold lived in that house until they died. Eva was ninety-six.

Can you imagine the power of a wand from the kitchen floor of that house? The love, kindness, and perhaps anger and angst, mixed with parents, children, grands, and great grands. If given the chance to make a generational wand, which is what I call barnboard, you should take it. The wand will give you reflective communication powers to connect to generations that you never knew. It can also be used for family births and blessings, passing its powers and energies on to another generation as it did to yours. The barnboard I own in my collection is one of four turned from a kitchen floor piece of an 1887 house in Piedmont, South Carolina. It has exceptional generational properties, and the owners of these wands are doing some amazing heredity and family magic.

As I teach in my seminars, there are three types of wands for southern magic: magnolia is for high plantation magic, dogwood is for crop magic, and barnboard is for conjure or root magic. Barnboard is the strongest of all the southern magic wands and should always be treated with respect for the lives that the wood has seen and influenced.

Hearth Wand

The hearth is a term we don't use much anymore. When witches and pagans were practicing in their huts and under the medieval radar of the authorities, the hearth was the central place of the home. It was the kitchen where you cooked your meals, the reading room after dark when there was only the fire of the fireplace, the heat for the house in cold weather, and the central area where women, and sometimes men, would gather to work their magic and their spells.

We have separate rooms now for these things. If we are lucky enough to have a fireplace, most of the time we don't use it and it's just a selling point for the house. Our fireplace is gas, and we don't light it more than once a year to make certain it still works in the event that the power goes out some dark and stormy night. However, it is still the central area to our house, as it is with many other houses I know of.

Above the hearth is the mantle. The mantle is where you usually put your most prized things since it is the place the eye is drawn to in a design. On our mantle we have some antique glassery that the cats would surely knock over and destroy if given the chance. There is also a hand-painted absinthe bottle from France filled with water from the supposed Fountain of Youth in St. Augustine, Florida, that we collected on a trip a while back.

However, it's the wand in the middle of the mantle that sets our hearth apart from many others out there. The wand is oak, and I know what I'm about to say later will slightly conflict with this, but bear with me. The wand is about fourteen inches in length with gears and brass on it. The stand is red cedar and grounds to the stone of the mantle. The wand points upward at a forty-five-degree angle toward the door in protection of anything that may enter to do us harm. The hearth wand is the guardian piece of the house.

But what if you don't have a mantle? What if you live in a small apartment with crowded shelves and limited space? Where is your altar? As a witch we all usually have at least one altar in our living area or bedroom. If the altar is close to the center of the house, then use that as your hearth. If you have your altar in your bedroom, as many witches do, then look for a place around the kitchen that you spend most of your time in. Even small apartments and houses have transition areas. Many are counters that separate the kitchen and living/dining room, and you may use that space. The key to a hearth is that it should be where you spend most of your time. That is where you place your wand.

Hearth wands are different than working wands. They are turned or created as wet and newly cut as possible. Therefore, they will work and dry and crack as they deem necessary for the house they protect. The reason they are created as close to the moment of collection as possible is that you want all the energy from the wand to be diffused into your house. Once the oils and saps and waters have dried, you have lost a powerful amount of energy.

The best hearth wand I have found is bay. It is a home wood, and between cooking and cleaning the wood and candles made from the leaves and oils bring prosperity during the Yule season and then throughout the year. Few candle companies are now making bay candles even though the trees are seldom used for anything else but leaves. Working with bay is lovely. The wood has an interesting gray that runs through the almost-white, clean grain. And the smell of the shop when you work bay lingers for days, providing a fresh and restorative air to the area.

The other very good hearth wand wood is red cedar. The red cedar is a money draw wood, and spells and rituals cast with a red cedar wand will go far to provide you with prosperity and health. Turning red cedar is as problematic wet as it is dry. The grain is rife with knots and shoots, and you must pay close attention to what you are doing or you'll snap the wand when it starts to bounce. Again, the air in the shop is therapeutic when turning red cedar, and I enjoy cedar anytime I get to work with it, whether it's the red or true white variety.

So why do I have a red oak Steampunk hearth wand instead of the two I just said were the best there were? The piece of oak I fashioned my Steampunk wand from was milled in my county. I saw the tree fall and planed it myself. I fashioned the pieces of the wand from brass stock and used the wand to cast my first Steampunk circle. It was also the first wand I ever turned on the lathe and is probably the best oak wand I've ever turned. Hearth wands, like other wands, often pick the hearth, and this one just fit well when I placed it there years ago to take a picture of it for Facebook.

There are no rituals or spells to call or cast when placing a hearth wand. That is up to you. Once you find your wand, don't be afraid to move it about until it fits. You'll know if it's a little out of place by the energy of the hearth. Once settled, you'll find that your house and your life will be a much more peaceful and grounded place to live and love.

Palm Wand

Palm wands are a curious invention that we can credit to the Victorian witches and those rich enough to support them. In the end of the Victorian era witchcraft was still illegal. Although burnings and stonings were no longer used as punishment for witchcraft, the caution that our sisters and brothers took was quite extensive, since the danger was still quite real.

Some of this changed in the last few years of the Victorian era, though. Many urban witches began carrying and using a smaller wand that would fit in their handbags or purses. These eventually became known as palm wands. These wands were crafted in the same way as the larger wands but were small enough to be easily hidden. As the witches became more emboldened, the palm wand became better known.

Eventually one or two caught the eye and the purse of the nobles at the time. These wealthy individuals would frequent their favorite witches for herbal remedies and fortunes, even though giving tarot readings and fortune-telling were still a punishable crime. As the wealthy met more witches and the witches met more wealthy patrons, palm wands became the gift of choice.

Finally, at the end of the era it would not be unheard of to see a palm wand carelessly slip out of a handbag at a dinner party held by a knight or dame of the realm. I say "carelessly" tongue in cheek because the lady in question would make certain the palm wand was seen just long enough to have people talking about her.

It soon became chic to be thought of as a witch or one who was a patron of a witch. These nobles or wealthy became the talk of their social circle, and the centerpiece of a group where dinner parties were organized and only the "right" people were invited. In the end it became a status symbol to know or be thought of as a witch. I wonder, how many of the wealthy bought their palm wands on the streets of London because they didn't have the money or the connections to be affiliated with a witch?

Part Two
Inorganic Wands—
Metals

We have spent many pages talking about organic materials. But what about the metals? I classify metals into three groups: royal, noble, and base.

Royal Metals

In magical work the royal metals are gold, platinum, and silver. They are the higher-end, very shiny metals most commonly used for crowns, jewelry, and coinage of great value. They also conduct energy exceptionally well. And they're the ones most people think of when dealing with adornments and filigrees to wands and other magical items.

Noble Metals

The noble metals are brass, bronze, and copper. These are the working metals of energy. They conduct energy very well and are found in all aspects of our daily lives, from water pipes to the coins in our pocket. The noble metals are less shiny than the royal metals but shiny all the same. We use a lot of the noble metals in Steampunk Magic, and they are the ones that are semishiny. Although only one metal, copper, is an element and the other two are alloys, they make up the second tier of wand metals and are therefore significant in their own right. Bronze is a combination of copper and tin, while brass is an alloy of copper and zinc.

Base Metals

Finally, we have the base metals. These are iron, lead, steel, tin, and other alloys, such as pewter. They are seldom shiny, and many of the base metals are used in conjunction with other metals to form alloys. They might conduct energy at some level or not at all, as in the case of lead. These are the working-class metals. They are your pots and pans, your nails, your batteries, and your cutlery.

Wands may be made of solid metals or a combination of metal, wood, and/ or crystal. Pure metal wands are very rare since metal is generally quite expensive, but there are some out there. Most metal wands currently being manufactured, if they are not add-ons to other wands, are tubing wands, either of all the same metal or of a combination of different metals. These are usually soldered, welded, brazed, or glued together to make one continuous piece that moves energy as other wands do.

Magical vs. Electrical Energy

I have mentioned common uses for metals for a reason. Every metal use is energy-driven. Cooking is energy. Electricity is energy. Flowing water is chi, or energy, since water is life. All metals move energy, and therefore these metals form an intricate part of your repertoire of tools.

At this point let us discuss energy in both its forms. There is the magical energy that we all use with our wands. This is a "feeling" as much as a manifestation of any physical force. Some will report that they can feel magical energy in their hands or up their arms when they pick up a certain wooden wand, or when they know that a wand is meant for them. I believe we all have had that feeling at least once if we have a wand that is ours. As I said previously, many authors tell young witches to wander about and find a branch or other item that "speaks to them" and that is the wand to choose. Yes, we also tell our students that, and we assist them in crafting their first wand; but do they understand the energy they are working with?

The second type of energy is electrical. While magical energy may also be electrical energy (because what else would cause the hairs on your arm to raise, or allow you to "feel" something but synaptic impulses?), this is an energy that is recordable. It is the force of nature in a demonstratable manner. Lightning is the most prominent example of demonstrated energy. When atmospheric conditions are right, electrical discharges of energy are released, and the lightning, either cloud-to-cloud or cloud-to-ground, are created. This electricity is the same energy that you may feel as either static or pulse energy in your metal wands.

Similar to the outside world running on a form of Gaiac electricity, our bodies run on electrochemical synaptic energies. The metals of our wands direct the electrical energies of the outside world and then align that energy to our nervous system's electrochemical energies. When both energies are in perfect alignment, magic is possible.

Royal Metals

Gold

SYMBOL: Au

ATOMIC NUMBER: 79

ATOMIC MASS: 196

GENDER: Masculine

PLANET: Sun

ENERGY: Projective

ELEMENT(S): Fire

GOD(S) REPRESENTED: Ra, Odin, Quetzalcoatl

GODDESS(ES) REPRESENTED: Tilo, Were

Gold is a transitional metal. It is, though, a masculine metal, unlike platinum, and it works better with male users. Gold has long been the standard of monetary value, and the term "gold standard" means that it passes the test that it is rock solid financially. Gold is impervious to nitric acid, which dissolves silver, and thus has been used to coin the phrase "acid test" as to whether something can stand up to pressure or rough service.

Gold is found in almost every part of the world. The gold in the United States is scattered from the Northeast to the far West and into Alaska, although it should be noted that much of the surface gold is from external sources to the earth. Meteorites striking earth have deposited much of the gold we surface mine. The rest is deep underground and found through shaft mining, similar to coal and other metals.

Gold as a metal for wands is almost as prohibitive as platinum. The price of gold makes a standard wand over $10,000 at today's prices, and that would not include the fabrication of the instrument. For that reason gold is also used sparingly as a trim or additive to other wands.

Magically gold is ideal for protection. As a sun metal, a wand of gold will protect its user, and the power generated by the wand channels the energies of the sun. Since gold is protective it is also defensive, and it will cast back spells at those who hurl them at you with great force. Gold is a money draw metal as well. Gold magnetic sand, although not gold or sand, is used as a replacement for the real thing in money and wealth spells. The gold in a wand will allow the user to direct the energy of the wand and the external powers into the charm that is worn as a talisman for wealth or riches.

Finally, gold is used for success spells. Like the money and wealth spells, the power of the gold in a wand will direct your energies to almost pinpoint direction and will speed up your success in whatever endeavor you are attempting.

Platinum

SYMBOL: Pt

ATOMIC NUMBER: 78

ATOMIC MASS: 195

PLANET: Earth

GENDER: Feminine and Masculine

ENERGY: Neutral

ELEMENT(S): Earth, Air, Fire, Water

GOD(S) REPRESENTED: Rugaba

GODDESS(ES) REPRESENTED: Gaia

Platinum is one of the rarest metals in the world. It is a dull gray in the ground and shines up to bright silver when finished. The largest deposits of the metal are found in South Africa, where approximately 80 percent of the world's supplies reside. Even though the heavy metal salts may cause health complications, the metal as a noncorrosive is strong enough to be a favored choice for jewelry and some wands.

Magically platinum is a neutral metal. As a transitional metal it works with all others and can be both receptive or projective, depending on the case. Further, the metal is cooperative to both masculine and feminine users and functions. Wands made entirely of platinum will be difficult to wield even though they are quite powerful. They are wishy-washy in their neutrality and therefore should be tempered with other metals or with woods or stones.

Combining platinum with other metals will enhance the metal that the platinum is added to. Likewise, if you use it as an augmentation to wood, the wood will have the prominent characteristics of the wand and the platinum will enhance those traits. Therefore, platinum may be used in positive or dark magic wands equally, depending on the witch or wizard's desires.

Silver

SYMBOL: Ag

ATOMIC NUMBER: 47

ATOMIC MASS: 107

PLANET: Moon

GENDER: Feminine

ENERGY: Receptive

ELEMENT(S): Water

GOD(S) REPRESENTED: Ge

GODDESS(ES) REPRESENTED: Diana, Isis, Ngami

Silver as a metal has a lot of number ones. It is the number one metal for electrical conductivity. It is the number one metal for thermal conductivity. It is the number one metal for coinage by sheer volume. And it is the number one feminine metal for wands. With all these number ones you can see why many wand makers use silver in their wands for either ornamentation or adornment.

Silver occurs naturally as a gray metal either by itself or with other elements. Similar to platinum, once it is melted, formed, and buffed it takes on a high-gloss shine that makes it perfect for jewelry and cutlery. Further, silver is ideal for electrical parts and other industrial uses that require high heat or high electrical passage.

Mythically, silver is associated with lycanthropic beings, mainly werewolves. As far back as 60 BCE the story of men being turned into wolves was told. Gaius Petronius was the first but far from the last to recount such wive's tales. The silver knife and bullet, however, were not added until the Victorian era, since silver was the metal of the moon, the cause of most lycanthropic changes.

Biblically, silver has always had a bad reputation. In Matthew 26:14 Judas agrees to betray Jesus for thirty pieces of silver. Since then silver has always been associated with betrayal and deception. In some vampire legends a silver cross is a sure protection against the undead; however, in some legends it just makes them angrier.

Magically silver is best used for emotional work and love. The metal is associated with all the Goddesses of love and lust and may be found on altars as far back as we have been making altars. Further, silver is useful for money draw spells due to its historic use as a coin through the ages. When performing a money draw spell with a silver wand or silver-adorned wand, make certain to use real silver coins, usually minted before 1965, in the spell.

Noble Metals

Brass

SYMBOL: N/A

ATOMIC NUMBER: N/A

PLANET: Sun

GENDER: Masculine

ENERGY: Projective

ELEMENT(S): Fire

GOD(S) REPRESENTED: Pan

GODDESS(ES) REPRESENTED: Gu

Brass is the first alloy in our list of metals. It is a combination of copper and zinc, and the proportions used are what makes brass soft or hard. Brass is found in many musical instruments, and in fact an entire section is named for the metal in orchestras. Brass is also used where friction without sparks is necessary, such as ammunition casings, fitting for flammable gases and liquids, and wrenches for machines where flammable sources are found.

Brass may also contain parts of lead, silicone, or manganese in varying amounts. Since the uses for brass are so widespread, each application will have its own formula. This causes brass from different sources to look significantly varied when placed side by side on a table. Therefore, be aware that as the properties of the metal change, your magical response may change as well.

Magically brass is excellent for Steampunk Magic. The conductivity, strength, and absence of friction make the wands and tools perfect for working on airships, the Steampunk version of covens. Brass wands are also very popular with other traditions since the grounding and connectivity of the metal to the earth elements allow for solid and successful rituals and spells.

Brass is excellent for money spells. Collect three brass coins (many of the Asian coins available at coin stores are made of brass), or cut a piece of solid brass rod into three thin wafers to approximate brass coins. Carry the pieces with you in a pouch with three tigereye stones. As you go about your day, think about gaining wealth and prosperity, and with the pouch you shall be more successful and thus wealthier.

Bronze

SYMBOL: N/A

ATOMIC NUMBER: N/A

PLANET: Mercury

GENDER: Masculine

ENERGY: Receptive

ELEMENT(S): Fire

GOD(S) REPRESENTED: Mars

GODDESS(ES) REPRESENTED: Athena

Bronze is an alloy of copper and other metals, usually tin. As a metal it is the most ancient of the warrior metals, and the Bronze Age of history was one of conquest and expansion due to the hardness of the metal over the softer brass and copper. Bronze is an excellent metal for use around flammable liquids and gasses due to its inability to spark.

In mythology bronze plays a role in the story of Jason and the Argonauts. Hephaistos created a giant named Talos to protect Zeus's lover, Europa, on the island of Crete. Talos was tasked with destroying anyone who approached the island, thus ensuring the safety of Europa. With the help of his wife Medea, Jason and his crew destroyed the giant by removing the nail in his head that kept all his powers within. In the movie of the same name, it is Poeas who removes the plug at Talos's ankle, thus draining him of his energies. Either way, the giant was destroyed, and Jason continued on with his quest.

Magically bronze wands are best for offensive magic. The alloy lends itself to taking the initiative in decision making, and with a bronze wand you may be able to seize control of the situation and lead the way to victory. However, in all offensive magical endeavors be aware that to strike first is not always the best maneuver. And to strike against someone who has done no harm to you will draw the wrath of the Gods down upon you and your family.

Copper

SYMBOL: Cu

ATOMIC NUMBER: 29

ATOMIC MASS: 63

PLANET: Venus

GENDER: Feminine

ENERGY: Receptive

ELEMENT(S): Water

GOD(S) REPRESENTED: Nyamia Ama

GODDESS(ES) REPRESENTED: Astarte, Ishtar, Aphrodite

Copper is the only element in the noble metals. As a building metal it is essential due to its carrying capability for electricity. Also, it is found in all houses as piping for hot water, and oftentimes cold, due to its ability to be sealed with solder to form watertight lines while still being somewhat light and safe for human use. Copper is also found in the body, and without trace amounts of it we would cease to function properly. Copper is found too in many commercial products such as herbicides, paint, building products, and artworks.

Historically it is interesting to note that the alchemy symbol for copper is also the symbol for the Goddess Venus, and the general symbol recognized as the symbol for women. That is one of the reasons copper so resounds with female pagans in this age, as previous ones. The copper conducts spiritual energy much as it does electrical energy. Wands made from copper—and many of them are fashioned from copper tubing or wrapped copper wire—form an extension of the arm, as any good wand should, and will move energy around a circle better than most.

In Steampunk Magic, copper wands are prevalent, and they are oftentimes embellished with other metals of the noble class. Many jewelry makers will use copper wire to wrap crystals and other talismans for sale and use.

Base Metals

Iron

SYMBOL: Fe

ATOMIC NUMBER: 26

ATOMIC MASS: 55

PLANET: Mars

GENDER: Masculine

ENERGY: Projective

ELEMENT(S): Fire

GOD(S) REPRESENTED: Mars, Thor

GODDESS(ES) REPRESENTED: Athena

Iron may be called the metal of the Gods since in early times the only iron available came from meteorites that fell from the sky. Early humans took this metal and formed tools, but that formation came with a price. Many cultures in the early history of our planet banned iron for its interruptive capability, and countries from China to Scotland have strict laws against using iron in religious rituals. One of the few exceptions is using iron as a defensive metal against exterior forces, but that is performed under extremely controlled circumstances.

Iron as a metal is soft and difficult to obtain without technological resources. The early pieces of iron were crude and poorly formed, with high proportions of other elements giving it different properties with each sample.

Notwithstanding these traits, iron is still highly sought after for many uses and in different forms as talismans. Using an iron wand would be anathema to early pagans, but iron now is being slowly accepted in some rituals and circles. Iron blades for athames and bolines are being crafted and sold, and iron pieces such as horseshoes and filings are used in luck and prosperity rituals regularly. Further, iron as a protection metal is now finding a new acceptance in pagan disciplines even though most witches still remove all iron from their bodies before entering circle.

It is a strange juxtaposition of superstition and acceptance for this metal, and most pagans have replaced the use of iron with steel, which is a harder substance, easier to obtain as a knife blade, easier to care for since iron rusts easily and heavily, and, most importantly, shinier than the dull iron and therefore more visible in public rituals.

Lead

SYMBOL: Pb

ATOMIC NUMBER: 82

ATOMIC MASS: 207

PLANET: Saturn

GENDER: Masculine

ENERGY: Receptive

ELEMENT(S): Earth

GOD(S) REPRESENTED: Pluto

GODDESS(ES) REPRESENTED: Hel

Nothing says "dense" and "of the earth" like lead. Of all the elements, lead is both one of the most used and one of the most deadly in the periodic table. As a benefit to man, lead is utilized in all batteries that use acid for power, as well as most early and some recent projectile weapons. The ability to easily smelt the metal and form it into whatever is needed has been the turning point to many scientific and military advancements. Lead is also essential in protecting against radiation, since it is so dense the deadly rays cannot pass to humans and other living organisms.

Lead is also, unfortunately, very deadly in its own right. Lead poisoning accounts for a large number of deaths yearly since lead was put into so many things as our civilization progressed. You can find lead in water main connectors, paint, ceramic glazes, toy soldiers, typesetting, early pewter, and batteries. The more we rely on acid/lead power sources, the more we pollute our environment with this element.

As a wand, lead is very poor for projecting anything. The metal is so heavy that to cast enough energy to send anything out would result in total exhaustion of the user. Therefore, magically lead is good for protection against almost all attacks and will ground your worst assaults and render them harmless. However, because lead is absorbed through the skin, you must be very careful when dealing with this metal. Use this wand only when absolutely necessary, and then only for short amounts of time. In a defensive mode, cast your circle of protection. Then, with the wand pointed downward, redirect all the negative energies that are being cast at you into the earth, where they may dissipate harmlessly.

Pewter

SYMBOL: N/A

ATOMIC NUMBER: N/A

PLANET: Jupiter

GENDER: Feminine

ENERGY: Projective

ELEMENT(S): Earth

GOD(S) REPRESENTED: Alaunus, Anextiomarus, Belenus

GODDESS(ES) REPRESENTED: Belisama, Sulis

Pewter is an alloy. It is a combination of copper, tin, antimony, bismuth, and, until recent centuries, lead. Lead is still used in non-food grade items, but for items that come in contact with humans or animals lead is no longer allowed in this country. There is a fine pewter company in Wolfeboro, New Hampshire, that makes Queen Anne Pewter that is not only safe for food use but keeps its shape and shine for years. I have a few pieces from the late seventies that I use every week, and it is as shiny and bright as when I bought it.

Pewter is often found in gift shops in wand shape. Many of the casting companies that make specialty items such as broaches and amulets will use pewter because of its low melting point, high shine, and ease of soldering to attach crystals and other jewels.

Magically a pewter wand draws from a number of sources. Because it is mostly tin, what is true of tin wands may be true of pewter ones. However, there is also copper in the pewter, so you may draw upon the copper's properties also. Pewter wands are good for heritage magic, the magic of the colonies. If you are looking toward your past, and you are from the coastal states that formed the original thirteen states of our country, then the pewter wand is for you. The power of pewter to draw back in time to that period when pewter was a common metal is essential for historic viewing or ancestral connection.

Lay a pewter wand on a photograph or sketch of a relative from your past on your altar. Make certain that the wand goes from the bottom left of the picture to the top right with the head pointing toward to top right corner. Also make certain that the wand does not cover the face of the person in the picture, even if you have to move the wand slightly. Then, in a darkened room, light a yellow candle placed at the top and just off the picture and concentrate on the image and the light. You should be able to make contact with that relative and ask what you need to know.

Steel

SYMBOL: N/A

ATOMIC NUMBER: N/A

PLANET: Mars

GENDER: Masculine

ENERGY: Projective

ELEMENT(S): Fire

GOD(S) REPRESENTED: Mars

GODDESS(ES) REPRESENTED: Athena

It's only fair that the next metal we talk about is steel, since it is an alloy of iron and carbon. Many think that steel is a relatively new invention; however, the ancients had steel possibly as early as the fourteenth century BCE. At that time the steel was a byproduct of the iron smelting when some carbon would mix with the iron to make a stronger metal.

Steel is not isolated to one specific location. The Africans had a steel furnace possibly two thousand years ago, and the Chinese used water to strengthen carbonized iron for a type of steel in the fourth century BCE. These, and the Greeks and Romans use of steel around the sixth century BCE, place steel all over the known world very early on. Steel began to reach its medieval zenith with the creation and production of Damascus steel, also called wootz steel. That dates to the fifth century CE and was refined by the Indian nations around Samanalawewa.

Steel now may be found anywhere in the world and is part of our everyday life. We use steel in our cars and trucks, we cook with steel pots and pans, our cities are created with steel, and our cutlery is usually stainless steel, a process of smelting the base steel with other elements such as chromium, nickel, carbon, titanium, copper, and molybdenum. When I was in my thirties, I worked in a foundry in New Hampshire for over two years casting steel and iron products. I loved the job because in the dead of winter when the temperature would hit minus 20 degrees you were always warm in the foundry. Unfortunatel,y during the summer the inner temperature would hit 150 degrees on the pouring floor and 200 plus as you got nearer the crucibles. However, the sight of molten steel pouring into molds was always worth the sacrifice of a few pounds of water.

In mythology and superstition, not always easily separated, steel and iron have a long history. The horseshoe is such an example. The iron or steel shoe must be used, found, and touched to be lucky. If the shoe is hung points up then it means luck will be held in the vessel. If it is hung points down then you will not be harmed. Either way, the steel or iron shoe will bring much luck to the house that has it on its front door.

Magically a steel wand will bring you great success in protection against negativity. It is said also that steel is a protection against Faeries, which may be quite bothersome at times during their forays into the realm of mortals. Using a steel hearth wand will keep all such beings from your door; however, it will also keep all beneficial Faeries and other fey out too, so you must evaluate what you are trying to protect against and determine if the expense of one over the other is worth the cost.

Tin

SYMBOL: Sn

ATOMIC NUMBER: 50

ATOMIC MASS: 118

PLANET: Jupiter

GENDER: Feminine

ENERGY: Projective

ELEMENT(S): Air

GOD(S) REPRESENTED: Jupiter, Zeus

GODDESS(ES) REPRESENTED: Hera

Tin, although often thought of with lead, is far superior to its heavier cousin. As a metal it has been used for millennia as the main component of pewter, a major drinking and dish metal. Tin, though, has also in the late nineteenth and twentieth century been the major canning metal for protection against spoilage in packaged foods. The term "tin can" comes from the fact that most cans were made from tin-coated metals since the metal fails to oxidize at the same level that other more porous and malleable metals do.

Tin is also a major player in the electronics industry, again with lead, as solder. Solder is the low melting point connector that holds electric wires together and also holds those wires to circuit boards or other metals. Solder has also found a use in Steampunk Magic, where brasses and bronzes are soldered together to form intricate wands on multiple metals. Solder is easier to melt than welding metals and is safer for those younger witches who should not play with high-temperature butane or propane fires.

As a magical metal tin is very good for money draw spells and other success rituals. For a money or success spell take your tin wand and cast a circle at the full moon. Then, with your wand facing north, place it over a large (at least one quart) vessel of water. Concentrating on your wand pointing toward the element of earth and the riches that lie beneath it, envision yourself receiving what you need within a specified time frame. Once the thought is securely put out to the Gods and Goddesses, close the circle and take the water to the edges of your property and sprinkle the water around the periphery. As you do that, continue to envision your success and rewards coming to you as you need. You should have results after that.

A tin wand will keep things contained, and when you need to organize your life or your sock drawer, a tin wand will lead you through the process with success. Cast your circle with your tin wand, and then pointing the wand toward the sky request from the Gods the power to organize and contain that which is being let loose or mingled. See in your mind how you wish to place everything in its place and where those items will be stored. Once you have that firmly in your thoughts, take down the circle and immediately start on your project. You will have clear thought and direction for whatever you need to work on.

Part Three

The Wands of
J. K. Rowling

Yes, I know J. K. Rowling probably doesn't have wands. However, her most famous protagonist does, and so do his friends and enemies. The wands that the characters have in the famous Harry Potter books are now known throughout the world, and it's important, as a reference point if for no other reason, to look at the wands and the characters that use them. Let's start with the boy that lived.

We first meet Harry Potter in *Harry Potter and the Sorcerer's Stone*. Young Harry is informed that he is a wizard and will be going to Hogwarts School of Witchcraft and Wizardry. On his journey there he collects his necessary supplies, including a wand. As Hagrid says, there is none better than Ollivander's, and he means the shop of Garrick Ollivander on Diagon Alley.

When young Mr. Potter enters the shop, Ollivander goes through the ritual of the wand chooses the wizard. He then presents Harry with a few choices, the first three being maple, beech, and ebony. I find these three choices important in the development of Mr. Potter since they are all good wand woods, but not what the chosen one would eventually need to defeat He-Who-Must-Not-Be-Named. The first wood, maple, is a good wood for furniture makers, candymakers, or those who fly—something Harry would do regularly as a member of the Quidditch team and then opposer of Voldemort. However, the power of the maple wand is limited in fighting evil, and it rejected Harry.

The Witch's Guide to Wands

The second wand was beech. Beech is also a fine wand, and it is very good for brewing and vintning, but it is less useful for combating evil on a daily or life-threatening basis. Finally, Harry is presented with an ebony wand. Now the ebony wand would be excellent for fighting, but ebony is a dark wood and more suited for those Harry will be combating; therefore, the wand refused him also.

Finally, the fourth wand, and the brother of Tom Riddle's wand, chooses Harry. That wand was holly. It is not surprising that the holly wand was the wand of choice for Harry Potter. Harry embodies all that is good and strong in the magical world. He protects the weak, rights wrongs, and fights dragons, monsters, and demons to save the world at the risk of his own life and those around him. The holly wand is best suited for those tasks. There is nothing negative that may be performed with the wand. It is incapable of harm to others unless they are evil, and the wand will never fail to support those with a strong and pure heart. Therefore, it was inevitable that when the holly wand chose Harry he would use that for good and righteousness.

Every hero needs a sidekick, and Harry has two—Ron Weasley and Hermione Granger. These two friends of Harry's, one pure-blood (Ron) and one Muggle-born (Hermione), accompany Harry through all the books and to the future, where Harry marries Ron's sister Jenny and Ron and Hermione marry. Much of the success of the Harry Potter books may be credited with the tensions—sexual as well as adolescent—between these three.

Ron's first wand is an ash. He breaks it by the second book and must replace it with a willow. Again, both of these choices show the character's development in the series and plays to Ron's strengths and weaknesses. Ash is a strong and solid wood; however, similar to much of what Ron has at Hogwarts, it is a hand-me-down from his brother, Charlie. Ash, though, is good for protection against lightning and flying, and it has been used by Celtic magicians for centuries. It is also a favorite of broom makers because the handles are strong and resilient.

The willow, on the other hand, is supple and not easily broken. After Ron's ash wand is destroyed by the Whomping Willow, it is ironic, or not so, that the wand that chooses Ron is a willow. The willow keeps Ron in good stead until he loses it to snatchers in the last book. It is not until Ron acquires the willow wand that he begins playing Quidditch, and it is probably not a coincidence that Rowling chose willow, which is used for cricket bats, to personalize Ron and his need for sports success.

The third member of the Harry Potter gang is Hermione Granger. Little is said of her wand except that it is vine. Most likely the vine in question for this wand is grape, but other vines have strong magical properties as well. The grapevine has a long and stellar history of civilizations and progress. Wine, made from grapes, has been the staple of countries and peoples since vintning was discovered, and when water was unsafe, wine usually was. The grapevine has for millennia been used as a symbol of Christianity and self-sacrifice, and those who harvest grapes are held in high regard.

Since grapevines must be quite mature to have a large enough trunk to fashion a wand from, and most vines at that age are essential to crops and produce, the vines are sought out and hard to acquire. For Hermione to have a vine wand is saying that the wand has seen something in the young girl that is not readily apparent, and in a number of places others say that she is the smartest wizard of her age.

Let us continue with the positive elements of the Harry Potter franchise. Next, there is Rubeus Hagrid. Hagrid's wand is oak. That makes perfect sense, since Hagrid is half-giant, half-human and reminds us most of the forestry God of many legends and traditions. The oak is a strong and solid wood that makes excellent wands for strength and stability. It is of Celtic origin magically, although many other cultures have taken the oak as their wand of choice. Many witchlings are provided with oak as their first wand project because it is forgiving to tools and strong but accepting to those unfamiliar with wand lore.

Next is Fleur Weasley (née Delacour). Her wand is rosewood. As we have discussed, there are a number of rosewoods available for wands. Most are good for board games such as chess, but in Fleur's case the counting and the accuracy of the movements of board games are translated to finances and the delicacies of transactions. It is not surprising, then, that with a rosewood wand Fleur would go to work at Gringotts Wizarding Bank.

Harry's father, James Potter, used a wand of mahogany. Mahogany is a wonderful wood to work with and has exceptional healing requirements. It is also good for cattle and dairy farmers, although little is known of James's past on the farm. Few use mahogany for wands, so it was an interesting choice by Rowling to include this exotic furniture wood in her list.

Lily Potter, Harry's mother, had a wand of willow. For all the healing and love that Lily had for her husband, her friends, and especially her son, the willow works very well and is a good fit for the mother of the chosen one.

Another friend of Harry's from the beginning is Neville Longbottom. He is, similar to Harry, an orphan even though his parents are still alive. Rowling once said in an interview that she had to leave the Longbottoms in the asylum. It would have been too easy to cure them at the end of the books. Neville's wand is cherry, which is the chosen wand for love and longevity. Neville is the unexpected hero that appears throughout the book to pull Harry along when needed. He is influential in taking out the bridge at the beginning of the castle siege and destroys the snake Nagini, and thus, the last Horcrux, paving the way for Harry to destroy Voldemort. Throughout all of this, include a run-in with the Evil Lord, Neville survives, and in the end he finds happiness with Hannah Abbott.

The final member of the good guys is Professor Minerva McGonagall. Her wand is fir, and this interests me most of all. The legend of the mouse and the bracts of the fir cones reminds me of her transformational abilities to become a cat. Chameleon-like abilities are found in those who use the fir wand, and the fact that McGonagall would be chosen by a shapeshifter wand is indicative of her early abilities being recognized by the wand.

Without an antagonist there can be no conflict. In the Harry Potter books that antagonist is Lord Voldemort. But before he was the Dark Lord, he was Tom Riddle. As Tom Riddle he carried a wand made of yew. The yew is an amazing wand. It is combat- and conflict-oriented due to the opposing grains within the tree that make it perfect for bows. It is also a deathly wood, since the bark creates a poison if taken in sufficient quantities, and therefore it may be used for good or evil.

The next most evil character in the series is Bellatrix Lestrange. To say she is mentally deranged is being kind. She is a psychopath who gloated about killing her own cousin, Sirius Black. She is the one who tortured to insanity Neville Longbottom's parents and swore Severus Snape to an unbreakable vow. It is not surprising that her wand would be walnut, since the juglans in the leaves will kill almost anything that tries to grow beneath it. The wood, especially the black walnut, is the perfect wand for someone as evil as Bellatrix. In the proper hands, the wand can do amazingly good deeds and spells, but as a wand of a psychopath, the choice works very well.

Draco Malfoy is another less-than-positive character who had a good wand choice. The hawthorn that Draco uses is said to be reasonably springy. That is the way hawthorn is. It is also an excellent wood for protection, which Draco would need as he tried to accomplish the will of the Dark Lord. The hawthorn also allows its user introspection and focuses the parts of his or her being that he or she wishes to strengthen. In Draco's case, he would have used the hawthorn to embolden his will to do evil, and that would have been necessary, since Draco was not necessarily evil. He merely wished to fit in somewhere, and within his strict, regimented family evil was the path taken.

Draco's father, however, was truly evil. Lucius Malfoy embodied all that was negative at House Slytherin. He was also the patriarch of the Malfoy family, a family that spanned centuries of pure-blooded wizards, and that plays heavily on his wand and its choice. The elm is the tree of Hel and deals well with the dead. Lucius would, as a Death Eater, be very cognizant of these traits as he wielded his wand. Additionally, the wood is good at organizing chaos and chaos magic, which would have been all around him during his time with the Dark Lord. It is also not surprising that in his time of need Voldemort would take Lucius's wand. The elm would call out to the Evil One.

I have yet to mention two wizards and one wand. The elder wand, originally owned by Professor Albus Dumbledore and taken from him by Draco Malfoy, is at the center of this entire story. Tom Riddle as Lord Voldemort wants the power of the wand more than life itself, and fortunately it costs him what life he had left to hold it and lose it.

Elder is a bad choice for wands. As stated earlier, the branches are poorly constructed for anything but growth. So for Death to break off a branch from a nearby elder tree would be poor planning. The wood, though, is good for spirit work, and sailors will hold part of their soul in an elder branch when they would go to sea, knowing they would not be totally lost if the ship went down. This is the fate of those who use an elder wand.

In conclusion, Rowling says in an interview that the elder wand knows no loyalty except to strength, and I think that is why Dumbledore had the wand so long and Draco couldn't control the wand before Harry won it from him. Dumbledore was a strong and powerful wizard. Draco was a weak-willed wizard who failed to be strong or evil or good enough for the wand to want to stay with him. Harry, though, was the strongest of them all because he was altruistic. He was good for the sake of humanity and was willing to die to save others. That kind of self-sacrifice is stronger than any evil imaginable.

The only major character whose wand choice remains a mystery is Professor Severus Snape. Snape is the tragic hero, doomed to eventual unrequited love and a conscience. He plays a good game at being loyal to Voldemort while working toward his downfall. He is evil, but only enough to get what he needs done; and he is good when it counts, as shown numerous times with Harry, whom he claims to dislike but saves on more than one occasion. I believe that the wand Snape carries is ebony. The ebony is a powerful wand that may be used for both dark and light magic. Snape would have been more than capable of controlling an ebony wand and working both sides of the fence, so to say, with it.

Conclusion

The blonde woman loaded the last box into the back of her SUV. It had been a very good event. Looking around, she could see a number of her canes and knew that three or four times as many witches were taking home her wands. When she turned to pick up the tablecloth that was at her feet, a young man walked up with a broad smile on his face. She had seen him all weekend. He was one of the volunteers who had made the event possible. One moment he would be cleaning out the trash in the porta-potties and the next minute he was carrying wood for the main ritual fire. Two nights ago, when she was coming back from a friend's tent at one in the morning, she passed him on security patrol. A few hours later at breakfast, he was there helping late arrivals unload.

"I finally got paid," he said, holding out his hand with two neatly folded twenty-dollar bills in it. "I want a new wand."

The woman pulled out the box with the wands and opened it.

"The wand chooses the witch," she said. "The witch does not choose the wand."

"Yes, ma'am," he replied respectfully. "I've been hearing you say that all weekend."

"Then be chosen by your wand, young witchling," she continued.

The young man put his hand into the box of wands, each wrapped in its own bag. After a few moments he withdrew one and handed her the two twenties.

She looked quickly at the bag and noticed it was a bur oak. An odd choice, she thought, but it was not her place to question the wands.

"This one," he said proudly.

The woman did not reach for the money. She closed the box and put it back in her van.

"You have paid enough for this wand," she said. "The wand may choose the witch, but that does not mean that all witches must pay for the wand that chooses them."

The woman tossed the tablecloth on top of the boxes and closed the hatch.

"I think one more person may need help," she said, pointing to a woman whose stroller was stuck in the deep sand of the road.

"Blessed Be!" the young man cried out as he ran to help the new mother.

"Bright Blessings," the blonde said after him, getting into her car and starting the engine. "Bright Blessings."

Acknowledgments

Once again I want to thank my wife Marla for being there as my rock, my sounding board, and my critic, in a good sense. She has knowledge that I will never possess, and when I needed guidance, she was always there.

I would also be remiss if I did not thank everyone who offered me wood, sent me wood, or suggested wood during the writing of this book. There are too many to name so suffice it to say that everyone's efforts were appreciated. I am still learning and collecting and can see doing so far into the future, so please don't stop asking me if I have this wood or that one.

Orion, my friend, thank you for your help with this book and for your foreword. I am pleased and honored that you carry my wands and I pray to the Gods and Goddesses that they never fail you.

I want to thank everyone out there who has sat through my lectures and classes during the production of this book. Your questions, comments, and assistance during those many hours in tents and hotel rooms and open fields allowed me to fine-tune this to where it is now.

Finally, I want to thank Weiser Books for trusting that this book was essential and for working so hard to get it on everyone's bookshelf.

Appendixes

Wands Listed by Use

Annoyance: Bamboo, Cottonwood, Padauk

Archery: Osage Orange, Yew

Barbecue: Mesquite

Blood: Cumaru, Redheart

Board Games: Rosewood

Breathing Difficulty: Mimosa, Rosewood

Brewing: Alder, Beech

Candy: Plum

Cardiovascular Health: Bloodwood, Cumaru, Redheart

Cleansing: Hemlock, Lavender, Maple

Construction: Bamboo, Hornbeam, Iroko, Zelkova

Control of Water: Alder, Birch, Cypress, Willow

Cooking: Alder, Bay, Chestnut, Hornbeam, Mesquite, Oak, Olive, Olivewood, Plum, Sumac, Tamarind

Courtship Conflict: Mulberry

Creativity: Laurel, Yellowheart

Cricket: Willow

Dance Magic: Mimosa

Dark Magic: Ebony, Poison Ivy, Walnut

Dealing with the Dead: Elm, Hickory

Deception Spells: Apple, Fig

Defense: Bay, Ebony, Gold, Padauk, Rowan, Sweetgum, Walnut

Deflection: Crepe Myrtle

Disruption: Yellowheart

Divination: Laurel, Sapele, Sycamore

Drumming: Iroko, Persimmon, Zelkova

Dyeing: Hackberry

Employment: Pecan

Energy Work: Ash, Copper, Sweetgum

Enhancement of Other Wands: Platinum

Escape: Crepe Myrtle, Zebrawood

Exorcism: Peach

Exploration: Goldenrain Tree

Faery Magic: Ash, Aspen, Elder, Hawthorn, Poplar

Failure: Yellowheart

Fertility: Fig, Pine, Rowan

Fighting: Blackthorn

Finance: Rosewood

Fire Ritual: Alder, Aspen, Olivewood (Black Ironwood), Sumac

Fishing: Bamboo

Flavoring: Acacia

Flying Safety: Maple, Spruce

Folk Magic: Barnboard, Dogwood, Magnolia

Forest Magic: Fir

Gaia: Basswood, Elm, Jatobá, Magnolia, Sumac

Gardening: Hornbeam, Leopard wood

Golf: Persimmon

Guidance: Osage Orange

Hallucination: Acacia

Healing (General): Aspen, Bay, Cedar, Cumaru, Dogwood, Ginkgo, Hackberry, Hemlock, Hickory, Lavender, Leopard Wood, Mahogany, Orange, Pink Ivory, Purpleheart, Rowan, Sapele, Sweetgum, Tamarind, Tulip Tree, Willow, Witch Hazel, Yellowheart, Yew

Healing (Stomach): Leopard wood, Licorice Root

Heart Health: *see* **Cardiovascular Health**

Heritage Magic: Pewter

Immortality: Basswood, Cherry, Olive, Peach, Pear

Intelligence: Chestnut

Invisibility: Fig

Jams and Jellies: Mulberry, Plum, Tamarind

Keeping Things In or Out: Chestnut, Osage Orange, Sumac, White Oak

Knowledge: Hazel, Rosemary, Wisteria

Longevity: Olive, Pine

Love: Apple, Basswood, Cherry, Copper, Fig, Hawthorn, Lavender, Maple, Orange, Peach, Pear, Silver

Lust: Basswood, Hawthorn, Maple, Pear, Silver

Machinery: Lignum Vitae

Marriage Conflict: Mulberry

Martial Arts: Bamboo

Memory: Acacia, Ginkgo, Rosemary

Menstruation: Bloodwood, Dogwood, Hackberry

Military: Blackthorn

Money: Brass, Eastern Red Cedar, Gold, Pecan, Pine, Silver, Tin

Music: Ambrosia Maple, Basswood, Canarywood, Ebony, Iroko, Monkey wood, Persimmon, Rosewood, Sapele, Spruce, Wenge, Zelcova

Norse Magic: Ash

Offensive Magic: Bronze, Cottonwood, Sweetgum

Oratory: Rowan

Order from Chaos: Elm

Organization: Tin

Pain Relief: Aspen, Willow

Plantation Magic: Dogwood, Magnolia

Positive Magic: Holly, Willow, Witch Hazel

Productivity: Hawthorn, Mahogany

Prosperity: Ash, Gold, Iron, Orange, Red Cedar, Sycamore

Protection (Chastity): Lavender

Protection (Drowning): Ash

Protection (Fire): Alder

Protection (General): Ash, Bay, Blackthorn, Bloodwood, Cypress, Ebony, Fig, Gold, Hawthorn, Iron, Lead, Locust, Oak, Padauk, Pine,

Purpleheart, Rosemary, Steel, Walnut

Protection (Insects): Canarywood

Protection (Lightning): Ash, Cherry

Protection (Snakes): Elder, Hazel

Reinvention: Blackthorn

Repellant: Crepe Myrtle, Osage Orange

Revitalization: Rosemary, Witch Hazel

Root Magic: Barnboard, Cypress

Santería: Iroko

Self-sacrifice: purpleheart

Sexual Prowess: Hawthorn

Sharecropper Magic: Dogwood

Skin Irritation: Padauk, Poison Ivy, Wenge

Smoking Cessation: Licorice Root

Smoking Food: Beech, Mesquite

Southern Magic: Barnboard, Dogwood, Magnolia

Speed: Zebrawood

Sports: Cherry

Steampunk Magic: Brass, Bronze

Strength: Hemlock, Locust, Oak

Survival: Palm

Tanning and Leatherwork: Olivewood

Thirst: Alder

Transitions: Persimmon

Travel Safety: Fig, Goldenrain Tree

Underworld: Elm

Unwanted Pregnancy: Lignum Vitae

Vintning: Beech

Visioning: Cedar, Chestnut, Cypress, Hawthorn, Jatobá, Mulberry, Rowan, Sapele

Water: Birch, Cypress, Willow

Water Safety: Birch, Canarywood, Mahogany, Persimmon, Teak

Weaving: Maple

Gods and Goddesses

A'as: Wisteria

Agwu: Purpleheart

Ala: Mahogany, Padauk, Purpleheart, Tamarind

Alaunus: Hemlock, Pewter

Amadioha: Mahogany

Amaethon: Locust

Amaterasu: Olive

Ame-no-Koyane: Goldenrain Tree

Ame-no-Uzume: Goldenrain Tree

Anextiomarus: Pewter

Aphrodite: Copper, Crepe Myrtle, Rosemary, Rowan, Walnut

Apollo: Bay, Hickory, Laurel, Olive, Palm

Apu: Lignum Vitae

Arduinna: Hornbeam

Ares: Holly

Artemis: Cherry, Chestnut, Crepe Myrtle, Cypress, Fir, Hazel, Mimosa, Oak, Palm, Tulip Tree, Walnut, Willow

Ashtoreth: Cypress, Palm

Asintmah: Hickory

Astarte: Acacia, Copper, Crepe Myrtle, Pine, Walnut

Atepomarus: Licorice Root

Athena: Bronze, Iron, Maple, Olive, Steel, Willow

Bacchus: Fir

Baldur: Eastern Red Cedar, Laurel

Bastet: Yucatan Rosewood

Bel: Blackthorn

Belenus: Pewter

Belisama: Pewter

Bolon Dzacab: Redheart, Yucatan Rosewood

Bran: Alder

Brigid: Blackthorn, Hawthorn, Oak, Rowan, Willow

Ceres: Bay, Laurel

Cernunnos: Oak, Pear

Cerridwen: Beech, Elm, Locust, Oak, Rowan, Spruce, Willow

Chantico: Sumac

Chaos: Yellowheart

Chiron: Tulip Tree

Cihuacoatl: Sumac

Cronus: Dogwood

Cupid: Orange

Cybele: Lavender, Spruce

Damara: Lignum Vitae

Danu: Holly, Zebrawood

Debranua: Zebrawood

Demeter: Pink Ivory

Denka: Olivewood (Black Ironwood)

Dian Cecht: Hemlock

Diana: Acacia, Apple, Chestnut, Cypress, Fir, Hazel, Oak, Palm, Silver, Walnut

Dionysus: Elm, Fig

Djunkgao: Teak

Eris: Yellowheart

Eros: Bay

Eshmun: Purpleheart

Fecunditas: Olivewood (Black Ironwood)

Fei Lian: Mulberry

Feronia: Olivewood (Black Ironwood)

Frey: Elder, Holly

Freya: Alder, Basswood, Birch, Hawthorn

Frigg: Ash, Hawthorn

Fujin: Mulberry

Gaia: Dogwood, Elder, Elm, Holly, Jatobá, Platinum

Ganesha: Wisteria

Ge: Silver

Goguryeo: Magnolia

Gu: Brass, Pink Ivory

Hae Sik Nim: Goldenrain Tree

Haoma: Purpleheart

Hathor: Crepe Myrtle, Sycamore

Haumia-tiketike: Leopard wood

Hebe: Rowan

Hecate: Aspen, Cottonwood, Hemlock. Locust, Rowan, Yew

Hegemone: Lavender

Hel: Beech, Eastern Red Cedar, Elder, Elm, Lead, Poison Ivy, Walnut, Wenge, Willow, Yew

Hera: Tin

Hercules: Olive

Hermaphrodite: Elm, Persimmon

Hermes: Yew

Herne: Oak

Hestia: Barnboard, Olivewood (Black Ironwood)

Horus: Olive

Huehueteotl: Sumac

Hygieia: Tulip Tree

Igbo: Padauk

Inari Okami: Mulberry

Inti: Bloodwood

Iroas: Olivewood (Bermuda), Zebrawood

Iroko: Iroko

Ishtar: Acacia, Copper, Palm, Willow

Isis: Fig, Fir, Palm, Silver, Sycamore

Izanami: Bamboo

Ixchel: Hackberry, Redheart

Jord: Magnolia

Juno: Fig

Jupiter: Cypress, Fig, Maple, Tin

Kichijoten: Mulberry

Kiribati: Sapele

Kokopelli: Monkey wood

Kumugwe: Barnboard, Hackberry

Kurupi: Jatobá

Lakshmi: Cedar

Lenus: Licorice Root

Liber: Plum

Loki: Eastern Red Cedar, Elm, Willow, Yew

Luison: Jatobá

Mahuika: Leopard wood

Mama Allpa: Bloodwood

Mapuche: Hickory

Mars: Bronze, Cherry, Hawthorn, Iron, Steel

Mary: Wisteria

Mboi Tui: Canarywood

Mercury: Hazel, Lavender, Pecan

Minerva: Ash, Olive

Momotaro: Peach

Morrigan: Cherry, Eastern Red Cedar, Locust, Oak, Willow

Nantosuelta: Lignum Vitae

Nei Tituaabine: Sapele

Ngami: Silver

Nokhubulwane: Pink Ivory

Nut: Sycamore

Nuxalk: Sweetgum

Nyambe: Padauk

Nyamia Ama: Copper

Obatala: Ebony

Odin: Ash, Basswood, Beech, Elm, Gold, Yew

Osiris: Acacia, Cedar, Cypress, Fir, Gold, Sycamore

Pachamama: Monkey wood

Paeon: Tulip Tree

Pan: Brass, Fir, Pine

Pasht: Yucatan Rosewood

Patecatl: Cumaru

Picumnus: Plum

Pluto: Lead, Poison Ivy, Wenge

Poseidon: Spruce, Willow

Priapus: Pecan

Prometheus: Wisteria

Qamaits: Sweetgum

Quetzalcoatl: Gold, Mesquite

Ra: Acacia, Cedar, Gold, Olive, Poison Ivy

Rhiannon: Maple

Roma: Olivewood (Bermuda)

Rongo: Leopard wood

Rudra: Crepe Myrtle

Rugaba: Platinum

Saranyu: East Indian Rosewood

Saturn: Dogwood, Holly, Mimosa, Tamarind

Sekhmet: Witch Hazel

Selvans: Sapele, Zelkova

Serket: Witch Hazel

Shiva: Cedar

Sita: Cedar

Sucellus: Hornbeam, Lavender

Sulis: Pewter

Tai Bitjet: Witch Hazel

Thor: Birch, Cherry, Hawthorn, Hazel, Iron, Oak, Rowan, Walnut

Thoth: Bamboo, Poison Ivy

Tlaltecuhtil: Mesquite

Tilo: Gold

Tu Di Gong: Ginkgo

Tyr: Aspen, Basswood, Cottonwood, Eastern Red Cedar, Holly

Ubasti: Yucatan Rosewood

Varuna: East Indian Rosewood

Venus: Basswood, Cumaru, Elder, Licorice Root, Maple, Orange, Peach, Pear, Persimmon, Pine, Plum

Vishnu: Walnut

Vulcan: Elder, Rosemary, Rowan

Wa-kon-tah: Osage Orange

Were: Gold

Winalagalis: Sweetgum

Wong Tai Sin: Ginkgo, Witch Hazel

Wuluwaid: Teak

Yamaya: Ebony

Yande Yari: Canarywood

Zeme: Zelkova

Zeus: Apple, Beech, Chestnut, Cypress, Hawthorn. Oak, Olive, Tin, Walnut, Willow

Zoran: Zebrawood

Sexual Energy

Acacia: Masculine

Alder: Feminine

Apple: Feminine

Ash: Masculine

Aspen: Masculine

Bamboo: Masculine

Barnboard: Feminine

Basswood: Feminine

Bay: Masculine

Beech: Feminine

Birch: Feminine

Blackthorn: Masculine

Bloodwood: Feminine

Brass: Masculine

Bronze: Masculine

Canarywood: Masculine

Cedar: Masculine

Cherry: Feminine

Chestnut: Masculine

Copper: Feminine

Cottonwood: Masculine

Crepe Myrtle: Masculine

Cumaru: Feminine

Cypress: Feminine

Dogwood: Masculine

Ebony: Feminine and Masculine

Elder: Feminine

Elm: Feminine

Fig: Masculine

Fir: Masculine

Ginkgo: Feminine

Gold: Masculine

Goldenrain Tree: Feminine

Hackberry: Feminine

Hawthorn: Masculine

Hazel: Masculine

Hemlock: Feminine

Hickory: Masculine

Holly: Masculine

Hornbeam: Feminine

Iroko: Masculine

Iron: Masculine

Jatobá: Feminine

Laurel: Masculine

Lavender: Masculine

Lead: Masculine

Leopard Wood: Masculine

Licorice Root: Feminine

Lignum Vitae: Masculine

Locust: Feminine

Magnolia: Feminine

Mahogany: Masculine

Maple: Masculine

Mesquite: Feminine

Mimosa: Feminine

Monkey Wood: Feminine

Mulberry: Masculine

Oak: Masculine

Olive: Masculine

Olivewood (Bermuda): Feminine

Olivewood (Black Ironwood): Masculine

Orange: Masculine

Osage Orange: Feminine and Masculine

Padauk: Feminine

Palm: Masculine

Peach: Feminine

Pear: Feminine

Pecan: Masculine

Persimmon: Feminine

Pewter: Feminine

Pine: Masculine

Pink Ivory: Masculine

Platinum: Feminine and Masculine

Plum: Feminine

Poison Ivy: Feminine

Poplar: Masculine

Purpleheart: Feminine

Redheart: Feminine

Rosemary: Masculine

Rosewood: Feminine

Rowan: Feminine

Sapele: Masculine

Silver: Feminine

Spruce: Feminine

Steel: Masculine

Sumac: Masculine

Sweetgum: Masculine

Sycamore: Feminine

Tamarind: Feminine

Teak: Feminine

Tin: Feminine

Tulip Tree: Feminine

Walnut: Masculine

Wenge: Masculine

Willow: Feminine

Wisteria: Feminine

Witch Hazel: Feminine

Yellowheart: Masculine

Yew: Feminine and Masculine

Zebrawood: Feminine

Zelkova: Masculine

Elements

Acacia: Air

Alder: Air, Fire, Water

Apple: Air, Water

Ash: Earth, Air, Fire, Water

Aspen: Air, Water

Bamboo: Air

Barnwood: Earth, Air, Fire, Water

Basswood: Air

Bay: Fire

Beech: Fire, Water

Birch: Water

Blackthorn: Earth, Fire

Bloodwood: Fire

Brass: Fire

Bronze: Fire

Canarywood: Water

Cedar: Earth, Air, Fire, Water

Cherry: Fire, Water

Chestnut: Air, Fire, Water

Copper: Water

Cottonwood: Air, Water

Crepe Myrtle: Air

Cumaru: Water

Cypress: Earth, Water

Dogwood: Fire

Eastern Red Cedar: Earth, Fire

Ebony: Earth, Fire

Elder: Earth, Air, Fire, Water

Elm: Earth, Air, Water

Fig: Fire

Fir: Air

Ginkgo: Earth

Gold: Fire

Goldenrain Tree: Air

Hackberry: Fire, Water

Hawthorn: Air, Fire

Hazel: Air

Hemlock: Water

Hickory: Earth, Fire

Holly: Earth, Air, Fire

Hornbeam: Water

Iroko: Earth

Iron: Fire

Jatobá: Air

Laurel: Air, Fire

Lavender: Air

Lead: Earth

Leopard Wood: Earth Air

Licorice Root: Water

Lignum Vitae: Earth

Locust: Earth, Water

Magnolia: Water

Mahogany: Fire

Maple: Earth, Air

Mesquite: Air, Fire, Water

Mimosa: Air, Water

Monkey Wood: Air

Mulberry: Air

Oak: Air, Fire

Olive: Earth, Air, Fire, Water

Olivewood (Bermuda): Earth

Olivewood (Black Ironwood): Earth

Orange: Fire

Osage Orange: Earth

Padauk: Fire

Palm: Air, Fire

Peach: Earth

Pear: Water

Pecan: Air

Persimmon: Water

Pewter: Earth

Pine: Air

Pink Ivory: Fire

Platinum: Earth, Air, Fire, Water

Plum: Water

Poison Ivy: Earth, Fire

Poplar: Air, Water

Purpleheart: Air

Redheart: Fire

Rosemary: Fire

Rosewood (East Indian): Air

Rosewood (Yucatan): Air

Rowan: Earth, Fire

Sapele: Air

Silver: Water

Spruce: Earth, Water

Steel: Fire

Sumac: Fire

Sweetgum: Fire

Sycamore: Air, Water

Tamarind: Water

Teak: Water

Tin: Air

Tulip Tree: Water

Walnut: Air, Fire

Wenge: Earth

Willow: Fire, Water

Wisteria: Air

Witch Hazel: Fire

Yellowheart: Earth, Air, Fire, Water

Yew: Air, Fire, Water

Zebrawood: Air

Zelkova: Earth

Celtic Oghams

Alder: Fern

Apple: Quert

Ash: Nion

Aspen: Edad

Birch: Beithe

Blackthorn: Straif

Elder: Ruis

Fir: Ailm

Gorse*: On

Hawthorne: Huath

Hazel: Coll

Heather*: Ur

Holly: Tinne

Ivy: Gort

Oak: Duir

Poplar: Eadhadh

Reed*: Ngeadal

Rowan: Luis

Vine: Muin

Willow: Sail

Yew: Idad

---

* Reeds, heather, and gorse are not vascular and do not make good wands; therefore, they are not covered in this book.

Index

THE WITCH'S GUIDE TO WANDS

About the Author

Gypsey Elaine Teague is the Branch Head of the Gunnin Architecture Library at Clemson University. She had advanced degrees in business administration, landscape architecture, regional and city planning, library and information science, and community mental health counseling. She is an Elder in the Georgian Tradition, Icelandic Norse, and the originator of the Steampunk Magical System. She is a noted lecturer and author with eleven novels, including *Three Years of Winter: Ragnarok Is No Longer a Myth*; *Fangs & Claws*, reviewed by Margot Adler in her Weiser anthology *Vampires Are Us*; and the seminal work on medieval mail, *Practical Chainmail in the Current Middle Ages*. For a hobby she builds early Norse farmhouse tools and wands. She may be reached at www.gypseyteague.com.

To Our Readers

Weiser Books, an imprint of Red Wheel/Weiser, publishes books across the entire spectrum of occult, esoteric, speculative, and New Age subjects. Our mission is to publish quality books that will make a difference in people's lives without advocating any one particular path or field of study. We value the integrity, originality, and depth of knowledge of our authors.

Our readers are our most important resource, and we appreciate your input, suggestions, and ideas about what you would like to see published.

Visit our website at *www.redwheelweiser.com* to learn about our upcoming books and free downloads, and be sure to go to *www.redwheelweiser.com/newsletter* to sign up for newsletters and exclusive offers.

You can also contact us at *info@rwwbooks.com* or at

Red Wheel/Weiser, LLC
665 Third Street, Suite 400
San Francisco, CA 94107